A Teaching Artist at Work

Theatre with Young People in Educational Settings

Barbara McKean

Heinemann
Portsmouth, NH

Heinemann
A division of Reed Elsevier Inc.
361 Hanover Street
Portsmouth, NH 03801–3912

Offices and agents throughout the world

Library of Congress Cataloging-in-Publication Data
McKean, Barbara
    A teaching artist at work : theatre with young people in
educational settings / Barbara McKean ; foreword by Maxine Greene.
        p. cm.
    Includes bibliographical references and index.
    ISBN 0-325-00882-5 (alk. paper)
1. Theater—Study and teaching (Elementary).   2. Drama in
education.   I. Title.
    PN2075.M39 2006
    372.66'044—dc22   2006005628

Editor: Lisa A. Barnett
Production service: bookworks, Lisa Garboski
Production coordinator: Patricia Adams
Typesetter: Gina Poirier Design
Cover design: Joni Doherty
Manufacturing: Jamie Carter

Printed in the United States of America on acid-free paper
10   09   08   07   06   EB   1   2   3   4   5

For

my parents, John and Eleanor

my brother, John

my pals, George and Louise

and

best friend, Kit

ontents

Acknowledgments

My thanks begin by crediting the wonderful teaching artists I have had the privilege of working with throughout the years. Gretchen Orsland is the best teaching partner I've ever had and a dear friend. Joseph Seserko writes music that makes any idea work on stage. Carl Sander, Suzanne Grant, and Volodia Vladamirov created plays and music that students loved to act and sing. Everyone at the Seattle Children's Threatre, the Seattle Peace Theatre, the Young Actor's Musical Theatre of Moscow, and the Children and Youth Theatre of Zurich opened my heart and eyes to what is possible when we collaborate across language, culture, and countries.

Of course, many thanks go to the wonderful and exciting students I've worked with throughout my teaching. They constantly surprise me with their energy and willingness to jump in and try out ideas.

Thanks to Lisa Barnett for believing in the need for this book and to my friend and colleague David Yarnelle for spending countless hours reading, rereading, and editing with me.

Finally, I am blessed with the love and support of a group of women we call the Hardy Girls. Through the years, we have resolved to keep our little community together even when separated by distance or death. To Kit Harris, Vicky Lee, Polly Conley, Beth Brooks, Rikki Ricard, Laurie Metzinger, Osani Shapiro, Kata Shapiro, and Shannon Christy, I give my everlasting thanks and love.

Foreword

This book offers its readers a sense of what it means to be a teaching artist in a school or community today. It is a story of a theatre artist committed to the translation of her talents, her creativity, and her imaginative powers into a practice intended to awaken young people to the wonder of theatre and to the techniques required to bring theatre pieces alive. Dr. McKean speaks to her readers from the heart of her experiences as actress, director, and designer. There is a lilt to her voice as she describes the joy and excitement associated with that work. And then, in the same voice, she tells of a dawning reflectiveness with respect to herself and her life project. Even as she has freely chosen a life in the theatre, she chooses herself as a teacher—a teaching artist.

Readers cannot but resonate to her account of her stepping into a new role, a professional role only beginning to be understood. Neither art teacher nor artist in residence nor visiting artist, she begins to view herself as a "reflective practitioner," informed and knowledgeable enough to feel at home in classrooms and to develop collaborative relations with teachers and students. Relieved of the competitive strains of theatre life, she feels keenly the values of participation and community that, for her, ought to be fundamental to the ends of education—ends nurtured by thoughtful engagements in theatre education.

Her story culminates in a professionalism exemplified by instances of practice: acting, writing, preparation of scenes, interpretation of monologues, movement, improvisation, vocal improvisation. The works presented are moving and impressive; their authenticity and tone somehow in harmony with the storyteller's voice. The story itself may open new windows for persons in search of life changes and, certainly, for those intent on enriching and humanizing what occurs in contemporary schools.

Maxine Greene
Teachers College
Columbia University

▌/ ntroduction

Connelly and Clandinin, in their book, *Teachers As Curriculum Planners*, state that "the more we understand ourselves and can articulate the reasons why we are what we are, do what we do and are headed where we have chosen, the more meaningful our curriculum will be" (1988, 11). This book is a reflection on my practice as a teaching artist. In it, I present a framework for thinking about the work of teaching artists and the personal and practical knowledge and experiences that comprise the artistry of the teaching artist at work. According to *Webster's Dictionary*, to reflect is to give back as in a mirror; to make manifest or apparent; to think quietly and calmly. The foundational purpose of reflection in education rests on the giving back of information in order to gain understanding of where we are and where we might want to go next. My hope is that this book gives back to others a way of thinking about the work artists do in education.

In *How We Think: A Restatement of the Relation of Reflective Thinking to the Educative Process* (1910/1991), John Dewey defined reflective thinking as "active, persistent and careful consideration of any belief or supposed form of knowledge in light of the grounds that support it" (6). The first adjective *active* indicates that reflection is far from a passive enterprise. Rather, a person chooses to reflect and is actively involved in the construction of those reflections. Second, *persistent* evokes a commitment to thinking deeply and to insist on it even when it might be difficult or contrary. Third, Dewey reminds us that reflection is undertaken with a conscious concern for one's self and others. *Any belief or supposed form of knowledge* suggests that reflection involves a certain amount of healthy skepticism and that there is value in suspending judgment in order to investigate possibilities. Finally, *in light of the grounds that support it* directly refers to the collection of evidence and criteria that informs the entire process of reflection.

Reflection, as Dewey also noted, should lead to action. Schön (1983) described this as "reflection-in-action" and characterized the person engaged in the process as a "reflective practitioner." Reflection in teaching leads to "professional artistry," or the ability to invent, question, test, and create new solutions in situations that are often full of surprise, ambiguity, or conflict (28–29). Such situations are the province of the teaching artist in education, inside or outside schools. Becoming a reflective practitioner is not only a desirable but also a necessary ingredient of a teaching artist's artistry and profession. Reflecting begins by clarifying one's own artistry. Each teaching artist brings his or her individual conceptions of knowledge, beliefs, and attitudes toward his or her art form and pedagogy. Teaching artists reflect on their experiences in the art form and in teaching to create a set of individual guiding principles and then use those principles to evaluate how well their actions in teaching fit their artistry. By considering their autobiographies as well as their practice, teaching artists strive for an artful combination of technique and decision-making that reflects their unique qualities as individual artists and teachers. Moving outward from artistry, teaching artists' choices in preparation and teaching are continually developed through reflective interaction with the particular situation, learning objectives, and group of participants.

The term *teaching artist* first appeared in the 1970s through the work at the Lincoln Center Institute and its arts education programs. When I began working in classrooms and in education programs with professional theatres, the term *artist-in-residence* or *artist-teacher* was used to set us apart from the arts specialists employed by school districts or artists who did not participate in teaching. Today, *teaching artist* has become the term used to describe the wide range of activities for those individuals who both practice their art form and engage in teaching others the knowledge and processes they employ as artists.

Teaching artists are distinguished from those who dedicate most of their time to teaching the arts in school and are licensed teachers and from master-teachers who share specific knowledge and techniques from their own work in a limited workshop-type environment. Teaching artists in education are expected to work as artists as well as invest themselves in the creation and implementation of projects in collaboration with other teachers or educational staff. The modifier—*teaching*—highlights the pedagogical nature of the work. It helps the individual conceive of teaching as the activity that modifies and drives the educational approach to the art form.

Theatre-teaching artists must be able to draw the students into imaginary worlds of play, engaging them in the theatrical process as a tool for exploration and learning both the art form and, by extension, other subjects. Theatre-teaching artists combine their theatrical and teaching knowledge, experience, and skills to create projects to introduce students to the world of theatre and enable them to participate actively in the construction of those worlds. In schools, theatre-teaching artists create spaces where teachers and students can envision a different way of learning and doing both theatre and other content areas in the classroom. In professional theatres, the teaching artist introduces students to the work of the theatre artist, creating a place where exploration of the art form can take place. In communities, teaching artists make instrumental use of theatre to explore and express issues of concern to both the local and global communities. This book offers a framework for considering what constitutes the artistry of the teaching artist's work and reflects on three projects in these contexts for teaching theatre with young people in education.

When I chose the word *work* in the title for *A Teaching Artist at Work*, I realized that I want to consider that word—*work*—carefully and with definition beyond what might at first come to mind. As a young adult, facing a life in which I would, like most adults, need to work to make my living, I came to the decision early on that whatever I chose for myself had to be something I felt passionately about and enjoyed doing. Acting was my first choice because when I was acting, my work was difficult and challenging, but infinitely rewarding. The work of acting was fun; it gave me joy; it connected me with others intimately; the meaning of my work was always revealing and always renewing. And through my work, I brought meaning and joy to others. When I started teaching, I found that the qualities I most enjoyed about acting were also true for teaching. The work was difficult, challenging, and infinitely rewarding. However, what I also discovered was that the work of teaching theatre had qualitative differences that were important to consider. The world of a working actor is often one of competition. We compete for roles, for jobs; we are subject to the whims and desires of the marketplace. We work to train our voices and bodies for performance in much the same way an athlete trains in sports. This is not what I have in mind when I consider the work of teaching theatre with young people. Here the work is not about training but education. It is not about competition but collaboration. It is about working to play with one another.

Herbert Kohl in his book *Growing Minds* (1984) introduced me to the Italian word, *giuoco*. In Italian culture,

> there is not a clear differentiation between work and play. The defini-
> tion of *giuoco* in a dictionary is play, but not in the recreational sense.
> *Giuoco* means extension of the lesson. Few lessons are complete with-
> out *giuocoing*. Contrast this with the American culture, where play is
> rigidly separated from work. Parents send their children to school to
> work, not to play. Teachers often support this idea and report the
> work schedule to parents at open houses and conferences. But play is
> an integral part of learning—not play in the recreational sense, but
> play as an outgrowth of experience . . . *giuoco* is pleasurable yet mean-
> ingful. (Tutolo, quoted in Kohl, 143–45)

What I want to capture in this book is this concept of *giuoco*, of playful work that fosters a sense of exploration and excitement in a place where teachers and young people work to play together in a spirit of cama-raderie and fun, a place where meaning is co-constructed, connected to the funds of knowledge each one of us brings to the work at hand.

Chapter One reflects on the history of artists in arts education and my own personal journey as a teaching artist to make visible my own experiences as an actor and teacher as they apply to my artistry for teaching. The work of a teaching artist is both personal and practical and is shaped by the individual experiences with the art form. How the individual interacts with and practices one's art form, how one learned the art form, and how one developed one's pedagogical knowledge and experience all influence one's stance toward artistry. In fact, one of the principal attributes of a teaching artist is that he or she is a working artist. The work one does and the choices one makes for teaching are critical to formation of artistry.

Chapter Two presents a framework for thinking about our work and the knowledge and experiences that inform the teaching artist at work. Calling on research in teaching, and specifically research on the knowledge base for teaching, I describe how the knowledge, experi-ences, beliefs, and attitudes of the individual teaching artist form his or her artistry. Within the overall framework, the individual's artistry is negotiated with others as they exist in different contexts and settings for the work and is applied to three central activities in education: prepar-ing, teaching, and reflecting.

In Chapter Three, I apply the framework to my own practice, relat-ing how my artistry drives my pedagogical reasons for preparing, teach-ing, and reflection. I offer a sample plan for preparing content and curriculum, descriptions and practical considerations for teaching, and basic assumptions driving my conception of reflecting. In Appendixes A and B are key exercises for teaching and tools for assessment and evaluation of student progress to aid in reflecting.

Chapters Four, Five, and Six present three projects created for specific settings and populations. Each project illustrates how I have applied my artistry in practice in collaboration with teaching artists, students, and others. Chapter Four illustrates a project set in a public elementary school in an urban city. Three teaching artists (two in theatre and one in music) worked with fifth-grade teachers, a reading specialist, and a music teacher to create a project that resulted in a theatrical and musical performance of the immigrant experience. The project illustrates the integrated curriculum approach many teaching artists employ when working in elementary schools. Through use of the textbook and materials in the teachers' social studies unit on the history of immigration in the United States and structured improvisations, music composition lessons, and creative writing exercises based on those materials, the teaching artists and students brought to dramatic life the content studied in the regular classroom. Examples of the script and lyrics from the songs are presented in Appendix C.

Chapter Five highlights the work of two theatre-teaching artists working in after-school and summer theatre programs hosted by professional theatres. Summerstage was a production program offered by the Seattle Children's Theatre. Begun in the mid-1980s, Summerstage was designed to provide dedicated young performers, ages nine to fifteen, concentrated study in rehearsal techniques, character development, and ensemble acting. The project presented in this chapter concentrates on the process of creating a performance project, using a variety of artifacts, scripts, art, music, and literature inspired by a central unifying theme.

A community educational theatre started by social activists and theatre-teaching artists is the setting presented in Chapter Six. The Seattle Peace Theatre was formed to explore how theatre might become the catalyst for teaching about and for peace with young people. The primary idea driving the work was to bring young people from different countries together to create performances that expressed the common hopes and concerns of young people faced with conflicts and issues both within their own country and across the world. In this project, the teaching artists and participants discussed and improvised ideas that were then scripted for rehearsal and performance by a professional playwright. The full script with song lyrics for *Boundless: A Musical Across Borders* can be found in Appendix D.

Chapter Seven offers a look toward the future by considering the work of teaching artists as a profession. Characterizing our work as a profession means we must not only engage in determining what knowledge and skills are necessary but also consider how members of the profession are selected and prepared. Recent strides in the development of teaching artists as a profession have led to an emerging focus on programs for initial preparation for teaching artists in higher education institutions. Professional arts organizations are focusing more effort on ongoing professional development of teaching artists as well. Building on cues from research in teacher education in general, this final chapter takes a look at my own efforts as well as those of others to identify some of the key components for initial preparation and ongoing professional development.

A Teaching Artist at Work introduces readers to a concept of artistry as it is applied to teaching theatre with young people in three particular educational settings. It does not include all of the work theatre-teaching artists do. Nor do I include the vast array of work done in other arts disciplines. It is a picture of my own work, informed and supported by others. At its best, the teaching artist's work is collaborative, not only with students but also with other teaching artists, teachers, students, and curriculum content.

In this book, I strive to articulate my own conception of artistry and practice with the hope that it will spark connections with other teaching artists and individuals who wish to create spaces where imagination and expression work together to create meaning. Maxine Greene reminds me of this when she writes: "What we are about can be, must be, life-enhancing, as more and more living beings discover what it is to make a shape or an image, to devise a metaphor, or to tell a tale for the sake of finding their own openings into the realms of the arts" (1995, 150). It is my hope that readers, new to or experienced with theatre-teaching artists, will find the framework and examples insightful and helpful as we continue—collaboratively, passionately, and modestly—to define our profession and explore our individual understandings of what it means to be a teaching artist at work.

7　A Look at the Historical and the Personal

From the early 1900s, classroom teachers and arts specialists, primarily in music and art, held the responsibility for bringing arts education into elementary schools. Secondary schools offered classes in music, art, and sometimes theatre, taught by teachers who were prepared in their content area. Arts organizations, such as museums, theatres, and orchestras, offered family programs and field trip opportunities for visits by schoolchildren on site. Occasionally, professional artists taught and performed in the schools. In the early twentieth century, the work of Jane Addams and the arts programs in the settlement houses lay the foundation for after-school arts programs for young people left on their own while parents worked. During the 1930s, the Works Progress Administration supported artists in university, school, and community settings. The Federal Theatre Project initiated a touring theatre for young audiences. The Junior League Association offered arts programs for children during World War II when so many adults were enlisted to help in the war effort.

By the 1950s, artists were hired by arts organizations to teach special classes for children or to conduct lecture demonstrations. Some organizations began to prepare curriculum and instructional materials that supported their own programs for schools. Arts organizations prepared touring programs for performances in the schools. The National Endowment of the Arts (NEA) and the Kennedy Center for the

Performing Arts, created in the 1960s, increased national funding and focus on education in the arts. Arts organizations and artists were funded to create, implement, and research programs in arts education. Artists were invited to work in schools for extended periods of time. These visits included working with students in the classroom, providing workshops for teachers, and giving performances and master classes for the community. The Alliance for Arts Education network, founded in the 1970s by the Kennedy Center, expanded the artists-in-the-schools programs nationwide. Arts and arts education programs in rural communities brought opportunities to smaller arts organizations and artists in rural areas to be paid for arts education work. State arts commissions, with the help of federal funds, also developed artists-in-the-schools programs, to connect local artists with local schools and organizations.

Beginning in the 1980s, cuts in federal funding to schools and the back to basics movement in education led school districts to eliminate many arts specialists from schools. These changes opened up more opportunities for artists and arts organizations to step in to fill the gap. The NEA acknowledged the increasing numbers of artists and organizations providing arts education in the schools by expanding programs to include professional development for teachers and administrators. Likewise, after-school programs in the arts flourished as parents, alarmed at the lack of arts education inside schools, began to seek out alternative experiences in the arts for their children.

The publications of *A Nation at Risk* (National Commission on Excellence in Education 1983) and *Toward Civilization* (National Endowment for the Arts [NEA], 1988) prompted a new round of school and educational reform that gained momentum in the 1990s. Educators and others realized that there was minimal agreement on exactly what all students should know and be able to do as a result of their K–12 educations. The task of identifying and garnering agreement on what were the core subject areas was the first hurdle. Through the persistent efforts of dedicated arts educators and educational arts organizations, such as the American Alliance for Theatre & Education, the arts (music, visual art, dance, and theatre) were included as one of the core subject areas. The next step in the process was to develop learning standards for their disciplines. National standards for what all students should know and be able to do in the arts were created in 1994 by the Consortium of National Arts Education Associations. Building on the national standards, state offices of education developed their own sets of standards for the arts, working with local arts educators, artists, teachers, and concerned citizens. The inclusion of the arts as a core subject and the development of national and state standards for learning in the arts was a huge victory for advocates and practitioners of arts education and brought the arts into the state and national spotlight.

The passage of the No Child Left Behind Act (NCLB) in 2001 (U.S. Congress 2001) threw a bit of cold water on the victory. The act is a massive document filled with legal language and "layers of parts, sections and subparts" (Chapman 2004, 4). In brief, the law requires that schools must "produce annual increments in test scores on statewide tests. The goal is to ensure that ninety-five to one hundred percent of students score 'proficient or above' in reading, mathematics, and science by 2014" (Chapman 2004, 3). As a result, schools—and teachers—are under considerable pressure to post yearly gains in student achievement in these three key areas.

The emphasis on reading, mathematics, and science has caused concern that other core subjects, as identified in the state and national standards, might receive less attention and instructional time in the classroom. The legislation itself does not exclude the arts or other core subjects, and government officials have been quick to point out that NCLB was not intended to eliminate arts programs. However, government funding of NCLB has been limited. Most of the federal funding has come from initiatives within the Department of Education and the NEA. And one hundred percent of that funding focuses on programs that rely on teaching artists and arts organizations to provide classroom teachers and schools with arts education. As a result, there is now a growing reliance of schools on artists and arts organizations for providing arts education as districts struggle with limited funds to meet the mandates of improving test scores in the primary areas outlined in the NCLB legislation.

During this same time, some educators turned their attention away from the education happening in schools to investigate what was happening in communities and youth organizations outside of schools. The President's Committee on the Arts and Humanities document, *Coming Up Taller*, written in 1996, recognized the wide array of these efforts as important sites for learning in the arts (Davis 2005). Local arts organizations, museums, symphonies, theatres, and dance companies offering education programs to young people had continued to grow steadily in response to the felt need from parents and others, acknowledging that education is part of the organizations' overall responsibility to the community. National sources of funding, private foundations, and local funding agencies providing monies in support of arts organizations began to require that arts organizations include education as part of their overall mission and programs. Artists and arts educators housed within these organizations are now seen as critical players to the accomplishment of the education goals of the organizations.

Beyond the arts organizations, community centers also continue to provide avenues for teaching artists to apply their work to these community-based settings (Davis 2005). Individual teaching artists often drive the curricular and the administrative engines of the programs offered. Indeed, most are artist conceived and managed. Some may offer arts programming within the umbrella of larger out-of-school sites, such as Boys and Girls Clubs, local community recreation centers, and the YMCA/YWCA. Others develop independent organizations and programs that use the arts as vehicles to address community concerns, such as violence, substance abuse, and teen pregnancy. Michael Rohd's Hope Is Vital program, as described in his book, *Theatre for Community, Conflict and Dialogue* (1998), is one example.

Personal Journey

The historical efforts for arts education and, in particular, for the development of the teaching artist as an active participant in education influenced my own journey. Like many theatre-teaching artists, I began as an actor, building my skills and knowledge in the theatre, first as a student, then as a working actor. The decision to teach was one that developed over time. The reasons for my own decision to teach mirrors what we know about choosing to teach in general. Some teachers say they always knew they wanted to be teachers. Others say they discovered their interest in teaching later on as they grappled with the decision of what to be when they grew up. Still others come to teaching after spending time in another career. The timing of when we decide to teach is related to our reasons for teaching and the images we project as teachers.

Most often our reasons are not singly defined but rather reflect a complex network of influences. Still, researchers in education conclude that the "most powerful reason is to work with or help other people" (Gerhke 1987, 8). This reflects the altruistic nature of the teacher's work and is often expressed as being called to teach in the same way as others are called to be ministers, doctors, nurses, counselors, or social workers. Teachers who feel called to their work think of themselves as people who have a stake in the future, giving the gift of knowledge and skills to future generations. For some, this calling is reflected in having had good teachers in their own lives and enjoying the environments of learning that schools and classrooms provide. For others, the calling may come from a feeling the educational system was or is less than what it could be. Their calling is one of making a difference, actively teaching to change the system or society, one student or classroom at a time. The calling may also stem from the subject area. Teaching is a way to continue to be involved with the subject they love and the joy of sharing that love with students.

Certainly not all teachers or teaching artists see their work as a calling. Work is work; some may choose teaching simply because it is convenient or available at the time and provides food for the table. And yet, as most artists and teachers come to understand, the money earned rarely reflects the extraordinary amount of time and energy the work requires. Although teaching can supplement an artist's income, as in master-teachers who give occasional workshops and classes, the teaching artist comes to see teaching as an integral part of his or her overall commitment to the art form. Commitment implies an obligation, a pledge both to one's artistic pursuit and to teaching that art form to others. The old, misused, and abused adage, "those that can, do and those who can't, teach," further complicates the effort. For myself and based on my conversations with other teaching artists, there is a fear that embracing teaching might lead to a lessening of focus or the perception by others of a diminished focus on our work as artists. Notwithstanding the stereotypes such thinking encourages, the ever-growing base of literature and research on teaching continues to point out that teaching is intellectually demanding in ways that are unique to the profession and require highly capable people whose skills and knowledge can lead them "toward a deep and sustained inquiry" into what it means to teach and what capabilities are required (Ayers 1995, 1). What is critical is whether the artist has interest, attitudes, capabilities, and the knowledge and skills for the profession of teaching as well as the interest, attitudes, capabilities, and knowledge and skills of his or her chosen art form.

Adding teaching to our work also has some powerful secondary motivations for the individual artist. Such things as "time compatibility" are important considerations for the teaching artist. An actor's employment in the theatre is sporadic. Even the most employed actors often find themselves with periods of time when there is no play to rehearse or perform. Unlike classroom teachers, teaching artists can control their own schedules. They can decide when to teach and when to work as an artist. In addition, the time structures of schools allow theatre-teaching artists to have nights and summers free for rehearsals and performance. Part-time teaching with arts organizations might also allow time for working with the organization as an artist. Second, teaching is portable. No matter where you live, teaching is always needed. This proves attractive to actors, especially because we must be able to move from job to job, often changing locations for long periods of time.

Others play an important part in deciding to teach. There is considerable evidence in education that teachers influence others in choosing to teach. They affect the choice by the ways in which they teach, the relationships they create with students and with the subject matter and/or learning in general. This does not mean that the influence is always positive. Although many teachers and prospective teachers say they were influenced by the love, respect, and admiration they had for their own teachers, others say they were called to teach because of teachers who had been indifferent, not caring, and/or abusive to them as students.

Parents also play a role in deciding to teach. The profession is one in which teaching often runs in the family. Because the occupation of teaching includes a large number of people and has such a historically high turnover, the possibility that someone has a family member who is or was a teacher is highly likely. But even if there are no other teachers in the family, the attitudes and values that characterize those who choose altruistic professions such as teaching are transmitted and reinforced by parents and family members. "The belief that good work is work in which we help others, regardless of money, is transmitted by many families" (Gerhke 1987, 11).

I view my decision to teach as grounded both in the subject—theatre—and in my desire to help young people learn. I love teaching. And I love acting. The two are linked in ordinary ways: Both are humanely collective, requiring interactions between people in intimate ways for specific purposes. Both require communicative expression of ideas, thoughts, emotions, and actions. They are also linked in extraordinary ways: Both are altruistic, devoted to the interests of others. An actor's devotion is to understanding of the characters that inhabit the world of the play. A teacher's devotion is to content and to the learning of that content by their students. Both engage in a process of finding out what makes those others (i.e., characters, students, content) tick. What are their interests, what are their hobbies, what do they know, what can they do, what do they need to know? Both acting and teaching embody a certain mystery. There is the miracle of moments shared, new meanings generated, and new insights into our own experience, something learned and experienced for the first time. For an actor, every night of performance is an opportunity for mystery. For a teacher, every moment in the classroom holds promise for fresh discovery.

As a young person, I decided to pursue acting because I felt most satisfied when I was acting. I would be dishonest if I did not admit that, in the beginning, I viewed teaching as something I could fall back on. I bought into the idea that teaching was somehow a "lesser" choice. I did not interrogate the complexity of teaching but rather subscribed to the ill-formed but popular notion that anyone could teach. I saw teaching as an add-on that would satisfy the fears of my mother, a teacher herself, and by the alarming reality that after college, I would need to make money. During my college years, I took classes in education and hated every minute of it. No way would I be confined to stuffy old theories of child psychology delivered lecture-style by those who I was convinced had not been in a classroom in years. My impatience for education was, fortunately, tempered by my experiences with exceptional teachers in theatre and educational theatre. Vern Adix, my professor in children's theatre, operated a theatre for young audiences company during the summer. University student actors were hired to teach summer classes and perform in the children's productions. In those summer classes, I witnessed firsthand the joy of playing theatrically with young people. And I saw the possibility of a profession wherein teaching and performing might be combined to form a particular career path.

Other teachers introduced me to alternative styles and/or kinds of theatre. As a young actor, I was always interested in demanding material. My high school English teacher introduced me to Shakespeare and allowed me to interpret Shakespeare's great women characters by acting out monologues as my final class project. One of my high school theatre teachers engaged a small group of beginning thespians in devising an experimental piece that combined mime, words, and music into what I thought was a stunning piece of physical theatre. It was not that I didn't enjoy acting in productions of any kind, but even in my early years, I suspected that I was most drawn to theatre that demanded more of actors and audience than a kind of passive entertainment.

Going to college in the early 1970s, I found that many others in theatre were also interested in creating theatre that disrupted traditional styles and presentations. I was introduced to theatre directors such as Peter Brook, Joseph Chaiken, Jerzy Grotowski, and Richard Schechner. I participated in company-created pieces of theatre that deconstructed the Western canon, taking plays such as *The Bacchae*, and reinterpreted them through improvisation. We created rituals based on the play that were performed in the audience space. As members of the chorus, we spoke and sang the text, often accompanying ourselves with drums and other instruments. An internationally respected dance/movement teacher, John Wilson, introduced me to new forms of physical theatre, creating a production of Shakespeare's *Measure for Measure*, told only through movement and music. For a graduate English course in dramaturgy and space, I performed Beckett's *End Game* in a handball court, Ibsen's *The Master Builder* on the roof of a high building, and Chekhov's *The Cherry Orchard* in a history museum. These early experiences opened my mind to possibilities for company-created theatre that viewed texts as malleable, as words, images, and sounds that could be shaped and reinterpreted by the artists working collectively.

My experiences with these alternative productions informed my decision to teach. Once out of college and auditioning for work, I discovered that most of the work I would do as a professional actor would not be with the experimental forms of theatre I had enjoyed in college. While I am always thrilled to work in the theatre, no matter the play or the process, I discovered that it was not enough. I needed to participate in collective experiments in theatre creating. As I began working with young people and other teaching artists, I discovered I could engage students in the very processes that I had found so thrilling in my early years.

Once I started working in schools, I also came to realize that theatre had something important to offer as a strategy of instruction in all classrooms. This was fueled by my own experiences as a learner in the system known as school. Learning to read had not been easy for me. I struggled with numbers and times tables. History was a boring string of facts. Sitting in desks for hours on end made me anxious and disruptive. Discovering theatre gave me a place to breathe and move. I learned to read because I wanted to interpret text as a character. History became alive in the context of lives lived and experienced in the world of plays. And as I began to teach, I found many students who struggled in similar ways. Theatre became a means for learning as much as a subject to be learned. My commitment to teaching soon included trying to make a difference in individual students' lives and in the systems in which students and teachers worked.

I was fortunate to come to my calling as a theatre-teaching artist at a time in our society when arts education was politically encouraged and financially supported. Through the 1970s, I found work, most often thanks to government funding, with small theatre companies across the western states. We produced children's theatre for performances in the schools, gave workshops for teachers and students, and performed contemporary adult plays for the communities in the evening. I attended actor-training workshops with respected artists and teachers, thus continuing my own development as an actor-artist. I was selected to be an artist-in-residence with state arts commissions and traveled the country, teaching in schools and helping to produce community plays.

My own development as a teaching artist in the 1980s continued when I joined the city-sponsored Poncho Theatre in Seattle as a teacher of after-school classes in theatre. When the Poncho Theatre reincorporated as the independent nonprofit, Seattle Children's Theatre (SCT), I continued to work as an actor, a teacher, and eventually as education director for a growing educational program of after-school and summer theatre classes for young people. After leaving SCT, I taught with the Seattle Peace Theatre and as an artist in the schools for the state and city arts commissions. I taught workshops for elementary classroom teachers and worked with the Washington State Alliance for Arts Education on arts education advocacy. During this time, I studied for a doctoral degree in curriculum and instruction with an emphasis on teacher education and the arts in order to understand teaching and learning better in general and to develop ways for investigating how the arts might inform the profession of teaching. My early experiences with school and with theatre continue to inform my artistry and the choices I make for the kinds of courses I wish to teach.

Educational researchers recognize that teachers' autobiographies and narratives play a significant role in understanding the knowledge and experiences each individual brings to teaching. How teachers use past experiences and knowledge to inform their present and future situations are part of the professional stories each teacher brings to the act of teaching. The artistry of the teaching artist depends on uncovering the personal and professional biography of the individual and is the first step toward understanding the unique qualities of our practice.

2 Building a Framework for Teaching

A Teaching artist assumes the mantel of a broader experience. Artists who teach primarily teach from their own experience, their own life, or their own professional process. A teaching artist primarily offers opportunities for others to make entry into the creative, artistic, historical and aesthetic experience of the arts."

(Burrows, quoted in Booth 2003, 4)

This definition, taken from the premier issue of the *Teaching Artist Journal*, helps to define the two broad concerns of the teaching artist: our content (the art form) and our pedagogy. In this chapter, my purpose is to delve into the knowledge and experiences in content and pedagogy that form my conception of artistry for theatre-teaching artists and place it within a framework for considering the relationship between artistry and the educational contexts and activities of teaching artists.

Teaching artists teach what they know and do; they are practicing artists. Knowledge and experience in their discipline and their continuing practice as members of that discipline place the art form at the center of the teaching artists' practice. For much of the history of artists in education, being proficient in one's art form was the primary expectation for becoming a teaching artist. For teachers in general, in the earliest years of schooling in the United States, no special preparations for teaching beyond knowledge of subject matter and some completion of school were needed. In secondary schools, it was assumed that a degree in the individual subject area was sufficient. In elementary schools, teachers needed to have completed their own education at least to the grade level they were teaching.

However, as the profession of teaching evolved, educators recognized that subject matter knowledge was not enough. In the mid-1830s, the preparation of teachers expanded to include study and practice specifically geared toward learning pedagogy as well as subject matter. The practice of teaching artists follows a similar, albeit a more recent, evolution. Today, those working in the field recognize that being proficient, even exemplary, in one's own art form does not automatically translate into teaching. As Burrows' definition indicates, the ability to offer "opportunities for others to make entry into the creative, artistic, historical and aesthetic experience of the arts," or what educators call pedagogy, is needed.

As teaching artists and those who work with teaching artists have taken on more of a significant role in arts education as a whole, and as pressure to measure and evaluate all educational efforts increases, it is not surprising that members of the teaching artist community would begin to "find solid stones of understanding to place at the foundation of our burgeoning profession" (Booth 2004, 211). A rubric for teaching artists, developed by the national network of Young Audiences (YA) to assess and improve the work of teaching artists, builds on the broad research on teaching to define eight categories for looking at the teaching artists' work. Rubrics by nature are designed to describe and measure through assignment of weight, numerically or descriptively (good, better, best), performance. Beyond performance, however, the categories for what is assessed offer a way to uncover the basic assumptions on the necessary body of knowledge and skills needed for creating common understandings and practices, a common language for continued development of the field.

The rubric uses the term *artistry* to describe the individual knowledge and experience with the art form. Pedagogical concerns include knowledge of learning theories, classroom management, curricular standards for learning, tools for assessment, and qualities of teaching, such as motivating learners and presenting material effectively. The YA rubric was developed primarily for those teaching artists working in schools and in relationship with classroom teachers and curriculum so the rubric also focuses on the relationship between teaching artist and teacher (Norman 2004, 219–26).

The TA rubric, as Booth suggests in his preface, is a "springboard for dialogue, self and peer assessment, and ongoing foundation building of a field" (2004, 213). The categories proposed lead me to consider a conception of artistry that includes both the individual's knowledge and experience with the art form and his knowledge and experience with pedagogy. Artistry rests within a circular framework in which the individual's artistry is negotiated with the individuals in specific contexts. The negotiated artistry is then applied to the central activities of education with young people: preparing, teaching, and reflecting (see Figure 2–1).

Artistry

My conception of artistry is based on education research and the conceptions of knowledge that are needed in teaching. Many define teaching as an art in that it "has rules, but knowledge of rules does not make one an artist. Art arises as the knower of the rules learns to apply them appropriately to the particular case" (Schwab 1983, quoted in Shulman 1986, 31). Going further, Sarason (1999) compares teaching with the work of performing artists to illuminate the creative and performative aspects of teaching. Teachers devise scripts or lesson plans and perform them with others. N. L. Gage, writing in *The Scientific Basis of the Art of Teaching* in 1978, states that teaching "requires improvisation, spontaneity, the handling of a vast array of considerations of form, style, pace, rhythm, and appropriateness in ways so complex that even computers must lose their way" (15). At the very least, the teacher is viewed as a skilled artisan or craftsperson, who builds a repertoire of skilled actions that is called on both in preparing for teaching and in the spontaneity of the teaching moment. When we compare these descriptions of teaching with descriptions of artists' practice (i.e., an actor improvising a scene; a musician building a repertoire; a visual artist blending form and color to create a painting), we find parallels between what we know and do as artists and what we know and do as teachers.

Content Knowledge

Research in subject matter knowledge for teaching provides evidence that content knowledge influences the level and quality of discourse in the classroom and how we critique and use the materials of our disciplines (Grossman 1990). Each artist brings his or her own understanding, just as any teacher of any subject matter does. One of the critical benefits of enlisting the aid of a teaching artist is the unique understanding of content the artist brings to the classroom or educational setting.

The teaching artist's knowledge and experiences with his or her art form include the major facts, concepts, and principles and the relationships among them, as well as the ways in which people carry out their

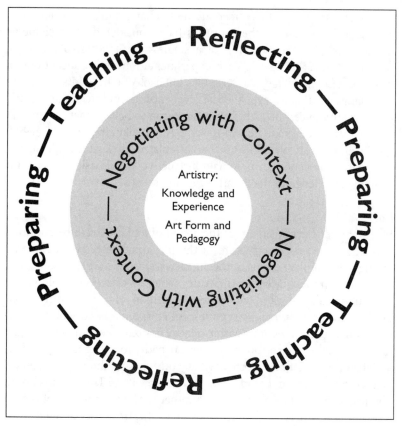

Figure 2–1. A Framework for Artistry in Education

work and evaluate the effects. What are the questions that guide exploration and inquiry in the discipline? For the theatre-teaching artist, such questions might include: What is dramatic action? How are plays organized? What theories of acting and directing inform the questions we ask when creating theatrical productions? What constitutes a "good" play? What defines a quality performance as opposed to a mediocre one?

These questions lead us, at the very least, to what I consider the foundational knowledge of a theatre-teaching artist, which is a basic understanding of dramatic structure and the six elements first described by Aristotle: plot, character, thought, melody, diction, and spectacle. These basic principles inform our work, if only to use them as an example of an oppressive theory, as Boal does in his influential work, *Theatre of the Oppressed* (1979). Boal's work illustrates that theatre is a dynamic and ever-changing art form, responding to changes in society at all levels. Theatre artists over the centuries have considered these elements not as some fixed conception of a single interpretation of dramatic structure but rather as tools for experimentation with conceptions of form, content, language, and space. As Michael Wright points out, given the changes in theatre over the last few centuries and most particularly in the twentieth century, "there is little reason to believe that theatre will retreat to the well-made play or to some Aristotelian framework" (1997, xiv). Still, the core elements, as first articulated by Aristotle, albeit presented in abbreviated form, remain instructive as the basic elements for content knowledge of the theatre-teaching artist.

Plot

Plot is the total arrangement of the action of a play. Not to be confused with the story line or structure of the play, plot describes the overall arrangement of the actions of the character(s) from start to finish. Story most often implies a linear structure, whereby one event follows the next in logical, and often, chronological fashion. However, stories need not be told through linear structures. An episodic plot structure reveals critical moments or actions within a story that are deliberately arranged not to follow a logical or chronological path from beginning to end. Wright (1997) defines plot as "what you wish to show an audience. Structure is how you intend to show that plot" (99). The point is not to define a single plot arrangement but rather to use the concept of plot to illustrate the variety of choices available to theatre artists to tell a story, and the conscious decisions on the part of those artists to fit the choice of plot to the story they want to tell.

Character

Theatre consists primarily of human action or personifications of non-humans in action, suggesting a close relationship between plot and character. Characters are "the material of plot, and plot is the form of all the characterizations, what the words and deeds amount to as a whole" (Smiley 1971, 79). Put another way, plot is "characters in action" (Chapman 1991, 23). All drama is primarily concerned with the relationship of human character to human action. Theatre artists are concerned with both what the characters say and what they do. "Character is not an adjective," Chapman points out. Theatre artists "must show the character acting in a situation that clarifies not only *what* the character is doing but *why*" (30). How characters speak and behave informs choices of language (what Aristotle termed *diction* and, to a lesser degree, *melody*) and physical expression through action. All characters are a "combination of someone's self-perception and other people's perceptions" (3). Thus, exploration of character involves close observation and reflection on one's own lived experiences as well as of those around us. Dramatic tension occurs when characters face conflict; however, drama is not "the conflict itself, but the changes [on the character] arising from the conflict" (5). Characters must speak and behave in believable and fully realized ways according to the circumstances of the situations within the world of the play.

Thought

A critical part of human behavior is human thought. The thinking of the character drives the spoken and the unspoken (often referred to as subtext) words, gestures, and actions. Complicating the concept further are those thoughts of the audience. "All the recognitions, realizations, and imaginings stimulated *by* the play are included in this category of thought" (Smiley 1971, 107). Audiences want to know what the play is about; what meaning they are to take from the play. Often, this is expressed as the theme of the play. Identifying and exploring theme sparks inspiration for the development of characters' thoughts that lead to action within or in response to the topic/theme. This exploration deepens understanding and breathes drama into what could become a relatively static and boring concept.

Spectacle

Theatre is a living art form. It is performed in particular and public settings. Aristotle used the term *spectacle* to refer to the visual elements that comprise the physical world of the play. Wright suggests the stage or play space is the "physical representation of potential . . . a space that contains possibilities, not realities: it is a place for imagining" (1997, 2). Even empty, the stage holds the promise of worlds imagined and actions undertaken. "I can take any empty space and call it a bare stage. A man walks across this empty space whilst someone else is watching him, and this is all that is needed for an act of theatre to be engaged" (Brook 1968, 9). The play's world is a "world selected, delimited and organized" (Smiley, 190), first by artist and then the audience. Audiences participate by "sustaining its agreement" to believe (or suspend disbelief) and enter into imagining the world as it is presented during performance. The degree to which audiences willingly participate and are actively engaged in the world represented in space is one of the measures of a successfully composed play.

Skills and Methods

The core elements constitute part of the language of theatre. It is a language learned through study (reading and seeing plays) and application. Content knowledge includes both the language of such key concepts as well as the language of the skills, attitudes, and dispositions for using that knowledge to create theatre. Knowledge and experiences of the skills include learned techniques and methods in the processes of playwriting, directing, acting, and design; and the creative discipline and collaboration required to accomplish a "construction of imagined experience" as Neelands (1984) describes the theatrical encounter. The theatre-teaching artist's knowledge includes techniques for acting, playwriting, directing, and design. For most theatre- teaching artists, foundational skills spring from a basic understanding of improvisation, as best exemplified in Viola Spolin's *Improvisation for the Theatre* (1963). Spolin's work was seminal in the development of improvisation. Her games and exercises form the basis for methods developed by acting teachers and directors whether working with young people in education or with others in professional theatre.

Pedagogical Knowledge

For the theatre-teaching artist, artistry is also informed by general pedagogical knowledge. Pedagogical knowledge includes knowledge of child psychology and learning theories, the organization of curriculum and methods of instruction, classroom management, and the philosophical and social aims of education. These areas of knowledge are directly connected to one another and are based on the personal and socially constructed beliefs and conceptions of the overall aims or purpose for education. Uncovering our aim for education in the broad sense allows us a kind of mantra or talisman that guides our pedagogical decisions and, ultimately, our artistry. But, educational aims and philosophies are not without dissent or disagreement. My conception of the general pedagogical knowledge for teaching artists is based on my own knowledge and beliefs about education informed by the literature on teaching in general and in the arts in particular.

Education is a particularly human and social activity. Societies and cultures around the world view education as a way to pass along the particular values, politics, and cultural practices of the individual society and culture. In the United States, one of the primary goals has been the education of citizens living in a democracy. To learn to be citizens in a democracy, learners must have ample opportunities to participate in democratic communities. Democratic communities have shared interests and ask for full interaction within the group as well as with other groups. Such interactions require flexibility and the ability to adjust to members' needs; they require skills to communicate with and relate to each other; they require critical thinkers who can reason through ideas and problems for themselves and ask questions in order to understand others and create consensus; and they require the ability to intuit and imagine emotions in order to care for themselves and for others. They are constructive thinkers. Such a person attempts to integrate personal knowledge with expert knowledge, to integrate the intuitive voice and the objective or critical voice. This view connects well with the aims of theatre teaching, wherein personal knowledge and expert knowledge combine to create opportunities for students to express their inner voices through character and use analytical processes to create dramatic structures for those characters.

Beyond the preparation of democratic citizens is the larger goal of what we value as members of the human race. We learn to be human by acting and interacting with other members of the human community. How we are treated, how we are socialized into the group, how our own stories are viewed by and told by others all influence the kinds of humans we are. Education is "an initiation into the skills and partnership of [a] conversation in which we learn to recognize the voices, to distinguish the proper occasions of utterance, and in which we acquire the intellectual and moral habits appropriate to conversation" (Oakeshott, quoted in Greene 1978, 78).

Creating humane and democratic classrooms rests on a conceptualization of learning that is based on constructivist learning theory. We know from information processing research that learning does not occur in a vacuum. Rather, when we learn something new, we connect it with what we already know in order to make meaning. And through those connections, we "construct" knowledge and skills, either replacing what we knew with what we learn or, more often, revising, expanding, and perhaps improving our previous knowledge and skills to accommodate the new ideas, concepts, techniques, and processes. This vision of learning deeply informs our vision of the other aspects of general pedagogy. If we embrace a constructivist theory of learning, then the ways in which we view curriculum and methods of instruction must follow suit.

From a constructivist view, curriculum is co-created. It is a negotiation between teacher and learner within the boundaries of the discipline and the developmental level of the learner. We often use the word *planning* to describe basic curriculum work. A teacher plans out the curriculum, for either a single lesson, a unit of lessons, or a year's worth of study. Embedded within the curriculum are assumptions about how to deliver the curriculum, as in methods of instruction. The constructivist approach views the planning process as one of *preparing* curriculum for teaching. Rather than writing extensive lesson plans prescribing particular moments of learning all learners will experience at relatively the same time, the teacher spends her time preparing content and materials, imaging multiple paths the learners might want to take. The challenge for the teacher is now one of creating worthwhile activities and selecting materials that engage and stimulate learners to build on what they know to learn something new. David Cohen calls this kind of teaching "adventurous teaching." In this vision of curriculum and instruction, the teacher is "a species of mental mountaineer, finding paths between innocent curiosity and the great store of human knowledge, and leading children in the great adventures from one to another" (quoted in Wilson, Miller, and Yerkes 1993, 85).

One of the most important areas of pedagogy is classroom management. In a constructivist classroom, collaboration is key. A view of classroom management whereby teachers take control of students in order to manage student behavior is at odds with the constructivist vision. Instead, the teacher organizes time and material to create spaces where teacher and learner negotiate the kind of space and the conditions necessary for everyone to engage actively and productively in the work at hand. The goal of classroom management becomes one of cooperation and not competition. Motivation rather than management becomes the central concern. From this perspective, teachers prepare to work with students by creating engaging activities that connect to learner interest and prior knowledge with the goal of inspiring them to want to do the work in ways in which everyone can succeed. The constructivist teacher shifts the focus from what learners ought to do to what the teacher can do to support learner development and help them learn. Such a perspective does not mean that expectations for behavior and performance are not present. Rather it means that the expectations are generated from the group and are related to the work that is undertaken. Research in these areas confirms that even children as young as two years old have the capabilities to work together for an intended purpose. Such research points to the cognitive and emotional capability of children to experience another's ideas and feelings effectively. When learners, even very young learners, are actively involved in creating and maintaining collaborative conditions for learning, rather than simply responding to an adult request for "appropriate" behavior, they take responsibility not only for their own learning but also for those of others (Kohn 1998, 42).

Pedagogical Content Knowledge

As teaching artists reflect on their knowledge and experiences with the art form and teaching, they begin to develop a new understanding of the content or artistry, similar to what Lee Shulman terms *pedagogical content knowledge*. Here our artistry informs how to teach our art form in ways that make it meaningful to our students.

> Within the category of pedagogical content knowledge I include, for the most regularly taught topics in one's subject area, the most useful forms of representations of those ideas, the most powerful analogies, illustrations, examples, explanations, and demonstrations—in a word, ways of representing and formulating the subject that make it comprehensible to others. Pedagogical content knowledge also includes an understanding of what makes the learning of specific topics easy or difficult; the conceptions and preconceptions that students of different ages and backgrounds bring with them to the learning of those most frequently taught topics and lessons. (Shulman 1986, quoted in Grossman 1990, 7)

Pedagogical content knowledge is divided into four central components. The first includes the knowledge and beliefs about the purposes for teaching a subject at different grade levels. These can be seen in the overarching goals for teaching a particular unit or lesson. The choices made are determined by the foundational understandings of the content, the understanding of child developmental theories, and the contextual influences surrounding the work. Teaching artists create goals for learning based on their own artistry, national and state content standards, the needs of the learners, and the desires/needs of others within the setting. These goals are the starting point in the journey. The how of the journey and the ways the goals change and evolve depend on the group doing the traveling. A theatre-teaching artist working with kindergarten students in a public school classroom might be asked to focus on the development of oral language skills and reading. Knowing the short attention span of kindergartners, the teaching artist might decide to use short poems that have accessible and enjoyable rhythms and rhymes to create a dramatic performance.

A second component includes knowledge of students' understanding, conception, and misconceptions of particular topics. Teaching artists must begin by finding out what students already know about a topic and what they are likely to find puzzling. Knowledge of child development and learning theories, as well as gathering specific knowledge of the particular students, informs and guides the teaching artist in generating the appropriate representations. A theatre-teaching artist understands that at the heart of acting is play. Tapping into the constructed worlds of make-believe of children is a natural way to introduce key concepts such as character and plot. Allowing students to construct the world of fairy tales or fables by acting out the stories might reveal the ways in which children naturally understand dramatic structure.

A third component is curricular knowledge. This refers to knowledge of curriculum materials available for teaching as well as knowledge of what students may have studied in the past, what content and curricula outside of the arts are taught and the relationships of those to drama/theatre, and the ways for organizing multiple strands of drama/theatre across a semester or yearlong study. The playwright and teacher Gerald Chapman (1990) begins his lessons by asking students what plays, movies, television shows they have seen. He recognizes that the materials of drama/theatre are not only published plays or textbooks on playwriting but also the stuff from students' own lived experiences. Theatre-teaching artists bring knowledge of contemporary plays that may be outside the typical canon of dramatic literature studied in school. They may be familiar with plays on teen issues and other issues pertinent to the students in the class. They rely on teachers to help them understand the materials within other disciplines, while at the same time adding their own knowledge and experiences with subjects such as history and the social sciences.

Finally, pedagogical content knowledge includes knowledge of instructional strategies and representations for teaching. This is where the working knowledge of the processes as a practicing artist is critical. For the theatre-teaching artist such knowledge includes techniques and processes for creating and communicating believable characters, improvisational exercises used to generate material, and community building activities that are integral to the collective process of creating theatre. The ability to adapt, revise, and create exercises depending on the needs of the situation requires the teaching artist to bring a rich repertoire of metaphors, exercises, and explanations that can be called on in a variety of situations and with a wide diversity of learners. A theatre-teaching artist working with young people in a middle school might create a series of exercises and improvisations that investigate the nature of being in the middle, caught between elementary and high school, between being treated as a child and as an adult, between friendships, and between parents who are divorced.

Norman, in her description of artistry for the YA rubric, states: "Quality arts and quality education share at least one common characteristic: both require balance between technique and creative impulse, between planning and improvisation, between respect for method and a taste for magic" (2004, 226). That last word—*magic*—is significant. I believe that artistry is the stuff of magic; those moments of transcendence and transformation, of that "wide awakeness." Maxine Greene so eloquently reminds us that Dewey instructed us that the opposite of aesthetic is anesthetic; that Dewey's interest in art as experience had to do with an interest in the ways in which art "concentrated and enlarged immediate experiences, in the ways in which they moved people to an imaginative ordering and reordering of meanings, to the effecting of connections, to the achieving of continuities" (1978, 171). Understanding the unique qualities and dimensions of our artistry is the first step toward building a solid framework for teaching.

Negotiating with Context

Our decisions for teaching are constructed based on our artistry in relationship to the needs of the specific localities and individuals within those locations. Teaching as a social activity is interdependent on a variety of other conditions and structures outside of any individual control. The context for teaching necessarily affects the nature of the individual project. Although context might refer to particular institutions, negotiation occurs in collaboration with people, not institutions (see Figure 2–2). Negotiation hinges on asking questions and working together to create shared understandings of such things as the content to be explored within the process, the expectations for learning and outcomes, and the philosophical foundations that drive our work together. Although the work is grounded in the individual's artistry, a teaching artist's work occurs within a variety of settings, all of which have their own purposes, populations, potentials, challenges, and constraints. The particular project is the result of extended conversations with those connected to the particular context.

Theatre is an eclectic and blended art form. It combines oral and written language with the visual and the physical. It is grounded in the human desire to tell stories. In the theatre, we tell those stories to one another through plays and performance. Theatre-teaching artists must communicate clearly what they envision in terms of their artistry in order to help the various partners find spaces for negotiation in light of each other's knowledge and experience. Although certainly not exhaustive of the many possibilities of settings for a teaching artist's work, broadly speaking, the teaching artist in education generally works within two contexts: inside schools and outside schools.

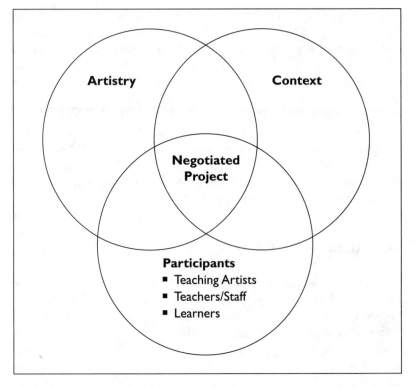

Figure 2–2. Negotiating Context

Inside Schools

In elementary and secondary schools, the most common relationship is between teaching artist and classroom teacher. Together, they develop projects that meet the educational goals set forth by the teacher, the school and district curriculum, and the state academic standards. The teaching artist brings his or her artistry and classroom teachers bring their knowledge and experiences of content and pedagogy. The collaboration with the teacher is usually temporary; the teaching artist will come into the daily curriculum at certain times and will not be present at other times. The teaching artist must integrate him- or herself into the school environment, recognizing that he or she is working within a whole school culture and curriculum. There are important questions teaching artists must ask to find their place. How does the classroom teacher view learning and students? What are the teacher's discipline and classroom management approaches, and what does the school require? What is the schedule of the curriculum and how does the classroom teacher see the work of the teaching artist fitting within the whole schedule? How does the teacher plan to participate while the teaching artist is working with the students?[1] The challenge for teaching artists is to find ways to be true to their artistry within the norms and ways of learning that have been set in the classroom by the teacher. For the collaboration to be a success, the teaching artist and the teacher must communicate clearly the expectations for working so these points can be negotiated throughout the preparing and teaching process. If students are to be asked to work in ways that are not standard practice in the classroom, then it is important to communicate those differences with the teacher, design a plan that accommodates for the differences while still respecting the authority of the teacher. Spending time observing the class at work beforehand helps the teaching artist to see not only how the teacher interacts with the students but also how the students interact with each other and the teacher.

Common also to the teaching artist's work inside schools is that the arts are viewed as tools for learning many skills and concepts beyond the art form itself. Teaching artists and teachers work together to find ways the artistic discipline can be a means for teaching across the elementary curriculum. Curriculum integration has a long history in education. The teaching artist can expect to encounter a plethora of descriptive terms used by teachers, such as *integrated studies, thematic instruction, holistic education,* and *interdisciplinary* or *multidisciplinary curriculum.* Without fully reviewing the definitions of these variants and the history of integrated education, the general view is that integrated curriculum refers to a method of teaching and a way of preparing curriculum so the discrete disciplines or content of subject areas are interrelated. Going further, integrated curriculum also seeks to integrate instruction, connecting the students' modes of learning, their own experiences and interests, with the strategies of instruction employed by the teacher. Integrated curriculum rests on the theory of constructivism so it is not surprising that teaching artists and teachers find this approach to curriculum well suited to meeting the goals of both the teaching artist and the teacher in terms of student learning. Theatre becomes one of the disciplines within the overall curriculum and the preparation

---

[1] State laws require certified or licensed teachers in the public schools to supervise students at all times; therefore, the classroom teacher must remain in the classroom. In the past, this has often meant that the teacher would sit in the back of the room, grading papers or doing other paperwork, entering the work only to enforce discipline in the classroom. Today, most teaching artists ask that the teacher participate in the activities with the students and even team teach the activities with the teaching artist.

focuses not only on finding connections between the theatre and the chosen content derived from other disciplines but also on providing opportunities for students to invest the curriculum with their own background, interests, and information.

Curriculum integration is also grounded in theories of intelligence. Most theorists agree that intelligence is multidimensional and not captured by any single ability. Howard Gardner's theories of multiple intelligences (1983) recognizes that individuals have different cognitive strengths and employ different ways of expressing what they know through the use of multiple symbol systems, such as language, numbers, or musical notation. These theories of intelligence have translated into educational practice by asking teachers to include multiple pathways for students to access content. Teachers are encouraged, for example, to provide opportunities to embody understanding physically, through movement and oral expression (theatre), or represent thoughts visually using color and line (visual arts) as well as encourage reading and writing words and using numbers. Integrated curriculum refers to an approach to both the organization of connected content and the instructional strategies for instruction.

Schools are complex institutions that fit within an even larger institution of government. There is a desire to see schools as small communities where everyone is working together to enact a commonly held set of objectives. The history of schooling in the United States and the research on education suggest that while no one would dispute this irresistible goal, little of it actually occurs. Longitudinal studies of school leadership and school-based innovations suggest that collegiality among teachers or administrators is much more "evanescent, volatile, and brittle than initial observations had suggested" (Little and McLaughlin 1993, 12). Recent research on teaching and teacher education has focused much more on creating positive conditions for collegiality and suggestions for policy that encourage collaboration both inside and outside of the school walls. Current political pressures threaten the collaborative climate by creating a competitive climate wherein teachers and schools must stack up against other teachers and schools as measured by student achievement scores on standardized tests. Making sure that all work done in classrooms is related to state standards and outcomes for learning has become a priority for most teachers and, by extension, most teaching artists working in schools. Furthermore, successful evaluation of teaching artists working in schools is often measured by their ability to contribute effectively to gains in student achievement scores. This has implications for the relationships forged between classroom teacher and teaching artist and for the design of arts education as a whole. It will be interesting to see how much the current accountability trend in education affects the work of individual teaching artists.

Outside Schools

Outside of schools, education is accomplished through after-school, Saturday, and summer programs that enrich and extend learning beyond the classroom. While the traditional institution of school garners the most focus from educators, studies show that schools account for only twenty-six percent of students' time. The other forty to fifty percent of time available to young people for outside activities includes participating in artistic activities, offered by teaching artists hired by either professional arts organizations or community organizations, employing teaching artists to provide arts education experiences. Recent research by Shirley Brice Heath found that arts organizations provide "fertile contexts for cognitive and linguistic development not available elsewhere for most adolescents" (Heath 1999, 20).

The purposes of these outside school programs are different from those of schools. For one, young people choose to attend. For another, the educational goals are much more specific to the art form itself but can include social, political, and cultural goals that reach beyond what occurs with the academic focus of schools. The contextual influences are just as great for the teaching artist working outside as they are inside the school environment. In some instances, the teaching artist may have greater involvement with the setting of the overall goals of the institution; in others, the teaching artist collaborates with the individuals within the organization to bring his or her artistry into harmony with the overall mission of the organization.

Professional theatres craft their educational programs based on the mission of the theatre and the targeted population. The individual teaching artist chooses to work with certain organizations based on his or her artistry and the individual's fit within the overall educational program. Many professional theatres offer educational programs designed to introduce young people to the processes of making theatre. Classes focus on skill building in areas such as acting, improvisation, vocal techniques, and movement. In this instance, the teaching artist narrows the scope of preparation to fit with the individual class. Other classes focus on performance, initiating young people in the process of play production. In some instances, theatres encourage working with prewritten scenes or full scripts, mirroring the traditional rehearsal and production process of the professional theatre. The theatre may choose scripts and scenes from plays selected from the theatre's own season of plays. Or it may choose to devise productions with the company, working to build a performance from within the process. Sometimes, the theatre uses the production classes as a way to try out script ideas that may become part of the professional theatre's season. How much freedom the individual teaching artist enjoys in crafting his or her own preparation for teaching varies from theatre to theatre.

Other theatre companies exist with the express purpose of providing opportunities for applying theatre to work with targeted populations in specific situations (i.e., in prisons, in juvenile detention, in homeless shelters). This work is often referred to as applied theatre. In applied theatre, companies "share a belief in the power of the theatre form to address something beyond the form itself" (Ackroyd 2000). Teaching artists working in applied theatre are dedicated to using education as a tool for personal and/or social transformation, and this is based on a view of theatre as "a form of knowledge; it should and can also be a means of transforming society. Theatre can help us build our future, rather than just waiting for it" (Boal 1992, xxxi).

When theatre-teaching artists work in applied theatre settings, investment in the overall goals is heightened. Clearly, as in any teaching situation, the teaching artist brings his or her individual artistry to bear on the process. His or her conception of artistry must also embrace the power of the medium as a vehicle for community action. As when working in school classrooms, in applied theatre, the teaching artist must closely observe and listen to the communities where the project occurs. He or she must become familiar with the issues that resonate with the experiences of that community and prepare his or her plan in order to draw from the participants the content and direction of the work. The theatre-teaching artist presents "a range of options from which decisions about necessary choices can be made" (Taylor 2003, 56). He or she offers concrete exercises and activities to provide structures whereby participants can step into a range of perspectives surrounding the human dilemmas the group has chosen to explore. The teaching artist working in applied theatre situations, Taylor reminds us, seeks to "generate pleasing and satisfying aesthetic work that permits a sense of group ownership...for the purpose of transformation change" (57). In applied theatre, the teaching artist enters into an ongoing and continual negotiation with the participants, ensuring that whatever choices are made arise from a commitment to dialogue and true partnership.

Whether inside or outside schools, artistry plus context inform the overall activities of preparing, teaching, and reflection. These activities do not exist in a linear structure; rather they are recursive in nature. Each one informs the other and leads to a continual renewal of ideas, decisions, and actions.

Central Activities: Preparing, Teaching, and Reflecting

Preparing, teaching, and reflecting constitute the central activities of the teaching artist at work. Taken together, these activities form a holistic curriculum, what Connelly and Clandinin term *curriculum as experience* or *something that is experienced in situations* (1988, 6). Educational situations are composed of persons located in a specific environment. These individuals interact with each other and the environment in certain dynamic ways according to the situation. All situations grow out of preceding situations and have a future, directed toward certain goals for learning. This conceptualization of curriculum assumes that the teacher is in control of making curriculum. Such a view seems particularly appropriate to the work of a teaching artist, whose purpose is to apply his or her artistry to a wide variety of educational settings and contexts. Shulman (1987) conceptualized these activities as a cyclical nature of "pedagogical reasoning" (15) that occurs throughout the preparing, teaching, and reflecting process, only to begin again either in the next lesson or for the next project.

The cycle begins with the teaching artist's understanding of artistry, negotiated by the needs and people within the educational context. It continues through a series of activities, critical transformations arising from the intersection between content and pedagogy, which provide opportunities for learning. These activities change and evolve through the interactions between individuals and the environment. Through ongoing and cumulative reflecting, teaching ends with new understandings of content and teaching. This model of "pedagogical reasoning and action" occurs throughout the three central activities in application to the task at hand, whether it is designing the overall project or the individual moments for learning within any given project. At the heart of the cyclical process is reflecting.

Reflection drives the overall practice. Our goal is to become flexible and fluent reflective practitioners throughout our careers as teaching artists. In preparation, reflection occurs in partnership with the other individuals connected to the situation. Working with a classroom teacher, the teaching artist reflects on the learning goals and content within the situation and the particular needs of the teacher and the school. Individuals within professional organizations reflect on the mission of the organization to ensure that the learning goals and activities selected align with the goals of the institution as well as one's own artistry for teaching. In community settings, teaching artists investigate the character of the neighborhood or community and the issues and concerns of the individual members of the community so that her plan reflects those qualities.

During teaching, the teaching artist reflects on the group responses and makes changes as the days unfold. Spontaneous reflective thinking occurs each time we teach. The ability to pick up subtle cues from students during the act of teaching and respond in appropriate and efficient ways is what Kounin (1970) referred to as *withitness*. Withitness allows the teaching artist to attend to individual students while reading the behaviors of the whole group and, at the same time, monitor and change his or her own behavior in response to what is happening in any given exercise. It is the first step in reflective thinking-in-action and is usually intuitive and sometimes emotionally driven. Participants may respond emotionally to a given exercise in ways not initially considered, and the teaching artist may decide to stop and allow for discussion. Or the teaching artist may react to a behavior or comment with a strong (positive or negative) emotional response. He or she may need to stop or slow down the exercise in order to reflect on what is occurring to cause this strong reaction.

The next step in reflection-in-action is to respond to perceived cues by gathering information and building a knowledge base to inform choices for action. Information comes from a variety of sources: content and methods books, other teachers, and the students themselves. Sensing frustration or boredom with the improvisations, the teaching artist might need to search for material that interests students. Perhaps students are having trouble mastering the discipline needed to do the work. The teaching artist might talk with other teachers or hold discussions with students to try to understand the underlying causes for the difficulty. Sometimes challenges arise due to contextual influences outside of the teaching artist's domain. He might need to attend a teacher's meeting or talk with others in the organization in order to understand the larger picture.

Once information is gathered, the teaching artist considers alternative choices for applying that knowledge to future action. Here again, the teaching artist calls on his or her artistry to invent creative strategies and methods that best fit the given situation, refining and adapting in productive ways based on continuous reflective thinking. Problems with discipline one day might lead the teaching artist to revise her plan and revisit the norms and rewrite ones that do not seem to be working. Student frustration might lead to altering the improvisations to include a variety of different texts not previously considered. She might decide to enlist the aid of another teacher or teaching artist in the next round of exercises. This is proactive reflection, considering options in light of the information gathered and experimenting with possibilities as the lessons proceed throughout the project.

At the end of a project, the teaching artist reflects on whether the overall goals of the project have been met. These reflections include assessing his or her efforts, in planning and teaching as well as assessing the participants. He or she takes note of what worked, what did not, and why. The teaching artist adds to his or her artistry new insights and through reflecting builds a teaching repertoire that in turn informs this artistry. New projects are begun with fresh eyes, renewed passion, and a thirst for putting reflections-in-action once again.

The term *assessment* refers to the process of collecting, synthesizing, and interpreting information. My use here is to refer to the assessment of student learning as it is accomplished by the teaching artist and participants. I also want to distinguish assessment from evaluation. We can assess, gathering information in nonjudgmental ways, before we evaluate. Gathering information without evaluating creates open spaces for exploration and builds trust within the group to take risks and experiment. Evaluation is the process of making judgments about what is good or desirable. Assessment and evaluation play an important role in reflective practice but should be seen as part of the overall reflection, not as something that stands independent of the preparation and teaching of a project.

The teaching artist wants to create a variety of tools for assessment along with what Robert Sabol (2004) refers to as a "menu of criteria" for the purpose of taking stock of and evaluating where we are in order to help us decide where to go next. Students participate in the construction of those tools and criteria so they can assess and evaluate their own progress in the art form and develop a critical eye for evaluating their own and others' performances. As Elliot Eisner (1971) suggests, the primary goal in assessment and evaluation "is looking back at ourselves to see how, from the information we secure about where [we] are, we can make the programs we provide more effective" (39).

And yet, contextual influences play a role in the teaching artist's practice for assessment and evaluation. The impact of the standards movement in education and the move to create standardized ways of assessing and evaluating student achievement of those standards has had a tremendous effect on the teaching artist's reflective practice. In schools, measurement of student progress is expected whenever a teacher devotes time to particular study. When a teaching artist partners with a classroom teacher, they must be able to articulate the learning goals for the project and demonstrate effectiveness by gathering evidence to show that students have reached those goals. Outside of schools, funding agencies and parents are requiring more and more organizations to demonstrate effectiveness. Program evaluations often depend on the ability of the teaching artist to collect evidence that can be measured using criteria that match the goals of the program in order to make claims about the success of programs to ensure further funding or enrollment. For most educational endeavors, inside and outside schools, local, state, and national standards provide partners with agreed-upon benchmarks for student learning. In theatre arts, such standards always include learning skills for improvising and scripting scenes. Standards also include knowledge of the concepts of character, setting, plot, costume, sets, and properties design. When creating integrated lessons, teachers and teaching artists call on standards in other content areas, such as key standards in social studies, writing, or science, to identify skills and content that complements the theatre project.

The development of standards in the core content areas not only provides common points of agreement on the goals for student learning but also informs the development of methods of assessment and evaluation. In this area, educators in the arts lead the way toward the development of what is referred to as authentic or performance assessment. In the arts, the ability to carry out an activity or produce a product to demonstrate knowledge and skills is a critical part of learning. Hence the need to assess and evaluate performance in situations that are authentic to the real-world situations of the artist led to the development of tools that go beyond the pencil-and-paper types of assessment commonly used in education. Alternative assessment strategies more closely aligned to the nature of the artistic process are necessary to capture fully the goals of instruction in the arts. Robert Stake (1975) termed this *response evaluation*, which is oriented to "what people do naturally to evaluate things they observe and react to" (14). What has resulted over the course of many years and many projects in arts assessment is the development of formative assessment and evaluation techniques connected to the curriculum and instruction goals and activities of the individual projects. Standardized testing may indeed become part of the overall strategy for capturing student learning in the arts, but the teaching artist will most successfully make his or her case for student progress and achievement through the use of multiple forms of assessment that are authentic to the tasks embedded in the project itself.

Many in arts education use a form of portfolio assessment, which has gained use in many other subjects as well. A portfolio is a collection of performances or products. In real-world situations, the portfolio is a vital and dynamic representation of an artist's work. Visual artists present a portfolio of their work to clients who wish to purchase their art. Performing artists present a portfolio of their work, shown either on paper, as in a résumé of productions, or through technology, as in video and/or audio recordings of their work. The portfolio represents a selection of their accumulated work, most often their *best* work, shown with the purpose of demonstrating their expertise in the art form. They might also include critical reviews of their work to demonstrate that others, knowledgeable in the field, recognize the quality of their contributions. They might include sketches and notes on the development of the work to demonstrate the ways they think about approaching their work.

When applied to education and teaching, the portfolio becomes a method for students to demonstrate their development as an artist. I like the term *processfolio* that Howard Gardner, from Harvard University's Arts Propel program, uses for this kind of portfolio (1996, 142). It is a variation of the portfolio. Rather than selecting examples of one's best work, in processfolio, students represent the evolution of their learning in the art form. The processfolio is a place where students can record their progress throughout the project: their initial ideas, false starts, pivotal places where an idea or skill gels, journal entries on their thinking about their work, critiques given along the way, documentation of the final performance, and plans for future inquiries or projects not yet undertaken. As a whole, the processfolio "not only documents the student's growth but aids significantly in the student's own reflexivity" (146). The teaching artist guides students in the development of their processfolios by providing prompts for reflection, by documenting performance, and by coordinating moments for documentation and critique along the way. She may also model the process by creating her own processfolio, an outgrowth of the reflective practice illustrated earlier, and sharing that with students as the project evolves.

Other assessment and evaluation tools include the use of performance tasks, which are then scored using checklists, rating scales, or rubrics. In this way, teaching artists can develop instruments that measure student progress and respond to the current calls for accountability in education. We have an obligation to demonstrate that our work is thoughtful, rigorous, and of high quality.

There are dangers of buying into what Maxine Greene calls the "cries of intense alarm" in education that seem to be driving the desire for quantifiable, scientific, evidence-based evaluation. Teaching artists and teachers do well to heed the warnings Maxine so eloquently states.

> It seems eminently clear that a return to a single standard of achievement and a one-dimensional definition of the common will not only result in severe injustices to the children of the poor and the dislocated, the children at risk, but will also thin out our cultural life and make it increasingly difficult to bring into existence and keep alive an authentically common world...through reflective and impassioned teaching we can do far more to excite and stimulate many sorts of young persons to reach beyond themselves, to create meanings, to look through wide and more informed perspectives at the actualities of their lived lives. (1995, 172–73)

We must think carefully about assessment and evaluation to make certain our designs do not exclude the multiple perspectives and diverse voices of the students we teach. We must also make certain our quest for evidence does not diminish or deform the very experiences with the art form we want to provide.

Taken together, the broad categories of preparing, teaching, and reflecting represent the enactment of a complete project. They are not fixed steps, but rather occur in different order and at different times. Each one is informed by the knowledge and experiences of the teacher and, in my case, by the artistry of the theatre-teaching artist.

Dewey tells us that engaging with art "involves a risk; it is venture into the unknown, for as it assimilates the present to the past it also brings about some reconstruction of that past" (quoted in Greene 1995, 171). The ordering and reordering keep us connected to the circle of activities in which teaching artists engage—preparing, teaching, reflecting, preparing, and so on. We rely on our artistry to ground us in past experiences and knowledge as we move forward in partnership with new contexts and new participants. We add to our artistry each time we engage in the process, while at the same time inquiring into what we know and believe. Teaching artists are mavericks. Each is one of a kind, taking risks, venturing into the unknown of adventurous teaching, and employing his or her artistry along the journey.

3 Applying the Framework to My Practice

My aim in this chapter is to reflect on my knowledge and experiences in theatre and pedagogy to illustrate how, taken together, my artistry informs my choices for the general activities of preparing, teaching, and reflecting. Specific examples of my artistry as negotiated within three different contexts are presented in Chapters Four, Five, and Six.

My passion for teaching theatre springs from the work I have done as an actor, exploring character and working within a company of actors to create a world of relationships between characters that are brought to life on the stage. My understandings of the elements of theatre—plot, character, action, thought, and spectacle—are built from the perspective on the individual actor working with others. My knowledge of theatre history and the broad canon of dramatic literature stems primarily from the desire to perform in those plays and to use the historical knowledge to build context for the characters I might play.

The knowledge and experience I bring to the teaching enterprise come from the following: working with skillful directors who guide actors and designers toward the creation of a whole; classes with insightful teachers who introduced me to exercises that have helped unlock my own potential for exploring first my own ideas, expressions, and emotions so that I could apply those explorations to creating a fully realized character on stage; books on theatre and teaching, offering new ways of looking at our work; and experience, from the actuality of doing the work myself so that the work is embodied within my being. In short, my knowledge and experience are grounded in performance. So it is not surprising that when I prepare for teaching, I am interested in developing work that results in a performance of some kind.

The goal of a public production does not always nor should it always accompany theatre teaching. There are plenty of wonderful examples of theatre teaching that focus on exploration through theatre for the purpose of using the process to explore themes, individuals, classroom content, and/or to build community, individual self-efficacy, and self-knowledge. Creative drama exercises offer teachers strategies to engage students in dramatic play in a variety of ways with no intent of public performance. Beyond creative drama, process drama work has also contributed a great deal to our understanding of the multiple ways drama can enrich education beyond the presentation of a play.

My introduction to process drama came from attending a workshop with Dorothy Heathcoate in the late 1980s. Dorothy is a leading figure in drama in education. She introduced the concept of process drama, a strategy of teaching whereby drama is used as a medium for exploring and imagining the experiences of other people in a variety of situations. The emphasis is on the experience and the participant's reflections on the experience. Cecily O'Neill points out that Dorothy believes that "process drama is never merely stories retold in action. Instead, it always concerns people confronted by challenging situations" (Manley and O'Neill 1997, 86). As the adult teachers gathered together for the workshop, Dorothy admonished us to stay on the periphery and silently attend to the relationships and work created between her and the young students brought in to work with her. I remember watching in awe as this master-teacher guided students not to create a "presentation" of any kind but rather to create a world, based on their ideas prompted by the question, What are we interested in today? Process drama employs similar strategies to the actor in rehearsal. Teachers and students work in role, taking on characters in order to live inside the drama they are creating. It relies heavily on the teachers' understanding of the dramatic form as a way to shape and guide the dramatic experience. And as Jonothan Neelands reminds us, it takes seriously the constructivist view of learning, whereby students construct with the teacher an imagined experience, bringing what they know into a hands-on process of inquiry and discovery (1984).

My own starting point is a blend of the process-oriented approach of drama with the product-oriented approach of theatre. My artistry calls on my knowledge of processes learned and used as an actor and those learned and used as a teacher. What has resulted is an approach that combines creative drama, improvisation, and devising. In contrast to improvisations in which actors perform scenes spontaneously on the stage with the audience, I apply improvisation as a technique for the classroom and/or rehearsal hall for the purpose of creating a performance that is then rehearsed and set before the audience arrives. This process of creating a performance through improvisation is sometimes referred to as devising—creating work that "has grown out of a group's combined imagination, skill and effort" (Kempe 2000, 64). Devised theatre relies on the collective ideas, knowledge, skills, and creativity of the participants to create the script for performance. Through carefully crafted improvisations and exercises, the director or teacher guides the group toward the realization of a performance for a specific audience. The characters, words, actions, and relationships created through the improvisations may be recorded by the members of the group and shaped by the group into the performance; or there may be a playwright (sometimes also the teacher/director) who translates the improvised work into a script.

The technique of using improvisation to create performance has its own theatrical tradition. From the sixteenth to the seventeenth centuries, Italian Commedia dell'Arte companies relied on broad physical gestures, stock characters, and improvised dialogue and clowning to create popular theatrical entertainments for large audiences. In the twentieth century, Meyerhold, Reinhardt, Copeau, and others embraced the traditions of Commedia and improvisation as a critical element of their styles. After World War II, devised theatre evolved in many directions, both in the United States and abroad. The shift in global consciousness led to a recognition of the world's fragility. The ephemeral qualities of theatrical performance even in its most traditional costume were given new clothes by injecting it with improvised spontaneity and radical departures from scripted stage reality. The experiments of theatre artists in the 1960s and early 1970s "rejected the traditional relationships between director, playwright and actor, and espoused the contrary approach in which a script evolves out of rehearsal rather than the other way round" (Smith and Dean 1997, 210). Such experiments were connected with a "collective democratic approach to the theatre" that explored the interactions between the actors, the environment, and the audience. Companies such as The Living Theatre, The Performance Garage, The Open Theatre, The Wooster Group, and others created a legacy of performed pieces that, although not necessarily scripted in a formal sense, celebrate the collective and creative nature of their enterprise. Theatre artists today, such as Mary Zimmerman and Peter Brook, continue to emphasize this collective approach in rehearsal while still asserting their individual artistry for the overall performance. Augusto Boal's experiments in breaking down the traditional roles between audience and actor further our conceptions of the collective possibilities for devising theatre.

What I love about this work is that it provides the actor with an active participatory role in the creation of the whole production rather than an interpretive role creating someone else's vision. In more traditional rehearsal processes, the actor can feel isolated from the playwright and director. This is not to say that in all traditional rehearsals of scripted plays, the actor is not allowed to have input into the overall creative choices. Of course, what makes all theatrical work so exciting is that exchange between artists in rehearsal and between artists and audience in performance. But typically, the working actor will find himself having less input into the creative concept for the production in most professionally produced plays. This is due partly to time and money. It is expensive to employ actors for the amount of rehearsal time it takes for collective creation. And it is partly due to the compartmentalization of theatrical roles: the playwright, the director, the designers, the actors, and the audience. Many people in the theatre prefer to work in isolation from others. The role of collaborator usually falls to the director. The play (and playwright if possible) fuels the director's vision. The designers and actors and ultimately the audience interpret that vision for performance. In devising work, every person in the process works together in both creating the overall vision and interpreting it for performance.

When I add my knowledge and experiences with pedagogy to the mix, I think back to what I loved as a student learning the art form. I want to consider the conditions that seemed to surround those times when I felt most successful and engaged with my own learning. Herbert Kohl (1988) advises teachers, when preparing to do theatre with young people, to consider the cast party. Cast parties are that wonderful release that comes after the hard work of rehearsal and first performance. Kohl starts with imagining ways cast parties can fail. Someone sulks in a corner because he did not get the part he wanted or her ideas were never heard. Someone feels that the teacher/director or members of the cast had treated her unfairly. Another felt the cast made fun of his mistakes. My positive memories of cast parties are those at which I am deliriously happy as a fully contributing member of the group. Together we celebrate the success of realizing our work for an audience. We laugh together about the evitable miscues or moments of near disaster.

A review of research on belongingness by Karen Osterman (2000) shows that students who experience a sense of relatedness or belongingness behave differently than those who do not: They display positive attitudes, and they are engaged with school and actively participate more in school and out-of-school activities. Imagining a successful cast party reminds me that my primary goal for teaching theatre with young people is to create a place where everyone feels as though he or she belongs. Furthermore, research on belongingness shows the positive attitudes gained are directly related to the "quality of the relationship they have with their teachers in specific classes" (344). Clearly, the responsibility for creating a sense of belonging falls on the teacher. Teachers do this by ensuring that everyone has the opportunity to participate and that everyone is involved in the choices being made.

I have participated in acting classes in which the teacher took us through a series of exercises designed to unlock students' potential for discovery with great success. At times, I left feeling a kind of vague dissatisfaction. I suspect my dissatisfaction arose because I had no participation in the choice of the exercises and little opportunity to share the discoveries I encountered as they occurred. I have also had the experience of working with other actors on productions whereby our postrehearsal times were spent grousing about the choices being made by the director and/or designers. Our complaints generally sprung from a perceived powerlessness we felt during rehearsals. There seemed to be no opportunity to offer our voices to the process.

I have also experienced times when I felt as though what we were creating, either for the stage or in the classroom, was greater than any one of us. My own ideas were made more powerful when voiced in relationship with other ideas and all were considered. Part of this had to do with the role of the individual director or teacher. We learn best from those who can skillfully guide others through the process rather than telling them what to do. Teaching (and I suspect good directing, although it seems at odds with what is commonly expected in professional theatre) requires what Neelands refers to as a release of ego (1984). We must separate our students from our own sense of self-esteem, success, or failure and attend to their needs instead of our own expectations of what we think they should do.

This stance might seem problematic for the actor-teacher. The stereotype of the inflated ego of the actor as star, center stage with all eyes on him, is at odds with the vision of the teacher as someone who suspends his or her own ego in service to the needs of the student. However, any actor can tell you who the generous actors in the business are. They are the actors who give unselfishly of themselves in service to the play and the production. These actors always listen to others on

stage. They are present in the moments of each rehearsal and performance. So as I consider teaching, I realize that the personality and skills
that I admire most in good actors (and directors) are those I admire
most in good teachers. And that the processes we learn in acting have
the power to help us be generous actors or stingy ones. As a theatre-
teaching artist, my role is to carefully observe and listen to the students
to construct experiences during which the students are center stage,
working with me to be the most generous actors we can be.

One of the educational claims of using improvisation in the performance building process is that it empowers participants to find their
own voice. My dissatisfaction in traditional acting classes and
rehearsals stemmed not only from the lack of a generous
director/teacher but also from a sense that even if our voices were
encouraged they would be discounted. It is not enough to be generous
in our teaching if that generosity is not authentic. Alfie Kohn (1998)
talks about what he calls *pseudochoices*, or those instances in the classroom wherein teachers offer empowerment under the guise of control.
"I see you've chosen not to participate" might be one pseudochoice you
could hear in a theatre class. Kohn also refers to the "engineering of
consent." I can envision this happening when a theatre-teaching artist
asks students to participate in deciding what the play is to be about,
when in actuality the teaching artist has already decided on the theme
of the play. This is not to say that we approach our work with no preparation or decisions made. Rather it is to be honest with what has
already been decided, what remains open, and that everything is "dis-
cussable" (258–65).

If I embrace the constructivist tradition of teaching and learning
and the aim of preparing students for living in a democracy, then my
goal of creating a community of learners also includes my valuing student choice and voice. My preparation must offer students the chance
to view learning as something they actively participate in rather than
some disembodied subject or exercise I am interested in teaching. It also
means that I must be open to a diversity of voices expressing ideas and
perspectives that may be very different from my own. With constructivism comes a pluralistic view toward teaching that embraces the culture, race, ethnicity, class, and gender of the students. Maxine Greene
says it best when she writes that when a student can choose

> to view herself or himself in the midst of things, as beginner or learner
> or explorer and has the imagination to envisage new things emerging,
> more and more begins to seem possible. A space of freedom opens
> before the person moved to choose in the light of possibility; she or

he feels what it signifies to be an initiator and an agent, existing among others but with the power to choose for herself or himself. (Greene 1995, 22)

Jerome Bruner maintained that "any subject can be taught effectively in some intellectually honest form to any child at any stage of development" (1960, 33). My knowledge of child development aids in the selection of material and activities, the amount of time devoted to each activity, and the structures of the lessons. However, my knowledge does not inhibit me from taking risks to challenge even young children to aspire to the highest levels of commitment and artistry. If I want to create spaces where students are encouraged to think for themselves and care about others, then my knowledge of classroom management is not a list of desired behaviors handed out at the beginning of our time together, but more of knowledge of what is asked for by the work we will be doing. My task is to use my knowledge to guide the group to construct together our norms for working and the ways we will manage those times when we fall short of the ideals we have set for ourselves.

Preparing

My reflections on my own experiences as a student and artist lead to the preparation of curriculum and instruction that stays true to my artistry, blending process and product to find methods of representing the content and the form in ways that are accessible to the students. Rather than beginning with a scripted play, holding auditions for parts and then proceeding to direct the play as happens in the professional work I participate in as a working actor, I choose to begin by building the community through investigation of the processes of acting, and slowly moving to the development of a piece of theatre that depends on the ideas and expressions that come from the work the group accomplishes together. My preparation leads me to create a plan for teaching, with objectives for learning and ways of assessment and a structured organization of time, but it will be a tentative plan, with spaces for evolution and change as the work progresses (see Figure 3–1).

The community building activities focus on setting up safe places for exploration and risk taking, which are so essential to creating a community of learners. I want to plan for activities that help students discover their own talents, expertise, and contributions to the group. I also remember students need to have a say in how our time together will be

Sample Plan

    Building Community

        Group Exercises

        Exploring Who We Are

        Setting Norms

    Skills Building

    Discussions and Selection of Theme or Topic

    Ways of Talking About Our Work

    Improvisations to Generate Ideas/Material

    Rehearsal/Performance

Figure 3–1. Sample Plan for Teaching

spent. Together, we must create norms for working together and develop strategies for monitoring and managing how we are doing and what might need to change.

I know we will have to do some skills building, developing flexibility and fluency with the basics of improvisation: accepting offers, going with our first ideas, listening to one another. We put ourselves in situations and work on developing characters, relationships, objectives, and settings (where). I use the acronym CROW to help us remember these four essential ingredients. Because I am interested in creating performances, I move to using improvisation to generate material and explore themes. The material is then collected into a loose script, and a more traditional rehearsal process begins to block and shape the piece into performance.

If I take seriously the notion of creating open spaces for expression and a place where student choices are valued, then I must also carve out time for discussion surrounding the selection of topics, themes, and/or material we will work with. We need to practice ways of talking about our work together so we can give positive feedback to each other throughout the work. My goals for moving to performance do not change, but rather I strive to apply my artistry to create a plan that fosters collective ownership of both process and product and communicates clearly what I envision for the project—how we will work together, the messy and experimental nature of the improvisation and devising process, the goal of performance—to find a balance between my artistry and the needs of the individual students and the context.

My theatre teaching with young people has occurred primarily in three contexts: elementary school classrooms, professional theatres for young audiences, and theatre programs organized by communities of concerned citizens. In the school classroom, the teaching artist has a responsibility to facilitate learning of specific content and skills, usually crossing several discipline areas, and thus must balance the desires of the students with the learning objectives created in partnership with the classroom teacher. My artistry finds the most authentic connections with the elementary school curriculum in language arts and social studies. When I begin preparations for content selection in conversation with the classroom teachers, my starting point is often the classroom materials, such as textbooks and trade books, and the specific learning objectives and standards within those subject areas. This enables me to select the most appropriate and most fruitful areas for integration with the theatre work I want to do with the students.

In professional theatre education programs, the teaching artist must find a balance between his or her artistry, the student's desires, and the mission of the theatre's educational program. Sometimes the goal is to prepare students for a visit to the theatre. In this case, the goal is not performance for the students but exploring theatre in order to respond fully to performance at the theatre. I find that process drama techniques often work well to meet this goal. After-school, Saturday, and summer classes usually include some form of performance. It is difficult to demonstrate mastery of theatre skills without performing. The content of the performance is determined either by the teaching artist ahead of time or in consultation with the students. My goal of performance can take form as a final sharing for peers and parents in the classroom or as a more fully realized production on the stage of the professional theatre.

In community settings, wherein theatre is a tool for exploring social and/or political issues, the teaching artist prepares with an eye toward the potential for introducing social or political change. In these contexts, the teaching artist creates open structures in which decisions about content and process come from the participants and are activated through reflective discussions with all participants throughout the process. When I apply my artistry to this context, my goal of performance is intended not only as a culminating expression of the participants but also as a means to invite the audience to consider possibilities for social and/or political transformation.

Teaching *Theatre is a profession of adaptation*

Two key assumptions guide my teaching. The first assumption is that everyone can participate in the theatrical experience. Talent does not determine participation but rather openness to the creative process. Because everyone is encouraged to participate, the development of the individual as a member of community recognizes that each individual brings complex and already present expertise to the work at hand. A second key assumption depends on the first. If everyone can participate, then the group determines the norms for working and the ways it will manage those occasions when the norms are not followed. In this way, the teaching artist and the group commit to a horizontal structure of collaboration whereby each member assumes a responsibility to respect and honor everyone's contributions throughout the project. The responsibility for ensuring the physical and emotional safety of the group and for managing the relationships, the methodology, and the organization of time and space for the work ultimately falls to the teaching artist. However, it is important that responsibilities are shared and agreed upon by all of the participants.

Practical considerations must be negotiated within the context of the particular settings. In theatre work, having a large, unencumbered space free from interruptions from the outside is the ideal. Often our work must be accomplished in a less than perfect space. In schools, desks and tables might need to be rearranged. In community centers, the space might be used for multiple functions and will require adjustments for the work. Noise levels of the work can also be a concern where the space is situated next to other classrooms or meeting rooms. It is important that the teaching artist consider the space carefully before the group arrives and communicate clearly to participants what is needed. Once the work begins, part of the group responsibilities is the care and management of the space. This also lays the groundwork for the creation of the performance space later in the process.

Time is another practical consideration. My rule of thumb is that one minute of performance requires a minimum of one hour of work. I have found this rule a useful way to discuss expectations within the context in terms of both the amount of time needed and the product of performance. In schools, the number of hours that can be dedicated to a theatre project is limited by other considerations of curriculum and school schedules. Outside of schools, there is usually freedom to spend longer, more concentrated blocks of time. Also, teaching artists are hired usually as independent contractors, paid an hourly wage or a lump fee, so it is important to negotiate the total amount of time to be spent before the project begins. It is also vital for participants to know how much time they are committing to in order to build trust and define expectations. Parents need to know the schedules for after-school, Saturday, and summer classes so they can plan and manage the various activities of the family.

The amount of time given to any one session depends on the scheduling within the given context and the age of the participants. Young children work best for thirty to forty minutes. Older students can sustain working for an hour or more. Telling participants how much time they will spend on a given exercise does two things: It sets the expectations and eliminates the worry that the exercise will go on forever. In any given session, it is important to leave space around the main activity for beginning and ending activities such as warm-ups, discussion, and reflection.

Another practical consideration is dress. Because theatre work is physical and requires the ability to move comfortably, some guidelines for dress are usually necessary. Rather than set a dress code, I find that the issue resolves itself quickly after the first few sessions of work. We can easily agree on wearing clothing that allows for movement because we have experienced what the work is like. However, another consideration around dress might include using it as a way to develop group identity. Questions concerning who we are as a group and how we might show that to each other and to outsiders can lead to group decisions concerning dress that go beyond the requirements of the work itself. We might decide to all wear white shirts when we work together. We might design a logo for a T-shirt that reflects our membership in this particular theatre tribe or company. Then as a signal that we are now working as a group, we might begin with a ritual of putting on our work clothes and end our sessions with a change back into our street clothes. It is important to stress that I am not talking about forcing everyone to dress alike. Although school uniforms have enjoyed recent appeal, Alfie Kohn and others suggest that the absence of any research supporting the use of uniforms indicates that adults base such decisions more on a desire to control student behavior than to build group identity. My purpose is not to control what students wear but rather to explore ways to express our group identity as set apart from other groups or occasions in which we participate as individuals outside of our group. Nor am I suggesting that we dress and undress as a group together (although it could be that a particular shirt or scarf could be added onto one's clothes as part of our warm-up). Rather, I am suggesting that when everyone enters the space dressed in a special way, we say to each other that we are now entering as a member of a particular group that has a

Flexibility is key

particular identity and purpose. Obviously contextual constraints and personal views will determine whether this is a practice the group wants to adopt. If appropriate to the setting, the teaching artist may suggest it. Ultimately, however, it is group decision as to how far they want to take the construction of a dress code.

Theatre-teaching artists bring their unique combination of exercises to their work depending on their individual artistry and the contextual purposes of the situation. There are many fine books of theatre exercises and games; I have listed some of my favorites in the project resource section of the bibliography. As theatre artists and practitioners, we learn strategies for teaching from reading and from our own experiences. As I consider my strategies for teaching, I return to my plan (see Figure 3–1) and adapt exercises to fit the needs of context changes with each teaching project. Some of the key exercises I use throughout my teaching are in Appendix A.

Building Community

Building community out of a group of individuals is always impressive and never easy. How does it happen? It involves paying attention to the dynamics of the group, watching and listening, acting when someone needs extra attention or when members are confused or troubled. It's about choosing and modifying exercises at the right time, matching the mood and the temperament of the group, and animating the imagination of participants in anticipation of the work to come. It is also about nurturing a sense of group identity, through shared experiences that build a sometimes-secret language between members.

In the theatre, the stage is the physical representation of the place where imagination takes form. So no matter if the space is not a stage but rather a room full of desks or tables or whatever, the space can be that place for imagining through the ways in which we interact within it. I begin each day by reinventing the space for theatre. It might mean everyone moves furniture; or it might mean that everyone gathers in the center of the large space. Whether or not the group adopts a dress code, creating a beginning and ending ritual for sessions is always a good idea. The beginning gives everyone a chance to check in with each other and put aside the concerns outside the work. The ending ritual brings the group together for acknowledgment of everyone's contribution to the day, to review goals for the next day, and to say good-bye.

Circles enable everyone an equal place where we can see everyone else. I like to begin community building with exercises that energize the group, are fun and nonthreatening, and introduce us to each other and to the work before discussing or talking. As I observe the students in the exercises, I start to take the temperature of the group. How comfortable are they with each other? Who is comfortable vocally and/or physically and who is less sure of him- or herself?

It is always important to introduce ourselves and talk about our interests and experiences with theatre. I like Gerald Chapman's (1990) advice to write the names on the chalkboard or a large sheet of paper and add notes of what they say about themselves and their experiences as you go. Writing the names with notes on the board gives weight to the introductions. It shows that the leader values what participants say and that what is said in our work together will be recorded and valued throughout the process. The notes introduce participants to the individual interests and experiences of each member of the group. In between the exercises, I ask students to continue to talk about what they know about the theatre, about acting, about movies, about television. As we talk, I add notes on the board.

This initial stage of community building includes getting to know each other so that we can identify what each of us brings to the work. Just as we have discussed what we know about theatre and the conditions for working, we also need to discuss what skills we bring. This step is critical because "in the collaborative process of devising drama, the work is divided between the participants depending on their individual interests, knowledge and skills" (Kempe 2000, 64). Will Weigler (2001) uses an "inventory of skills" worksheet to uncover the wide range of skills individuals bring to the process. As he points out, "invariably, participants will possess a high degree of physical ability in one thing or another outside the realm of what are considered theatre skills" (18). By listing out the kinds of physical, vocal, and visual skills we can do, along with the family and cultural traditions that we know, we make visible our potential contributions to the group.

Another key ingredient for building community is the consideration of what conditions are needed for us to feel comfortable and supported as we continue. By asking what conditions are necessary for our work together, we can create norms for working (see Figure 3–2). These norms or ground rules make public our shared agreements for how we will approach and manage our time together. The teaching artist contributes to the discussion as someone who has done the work before and has knowledge of what is necessary. The task is to connect what students know or suspect might be needed, based on previous experiences and the exercises just accomplished, to the process of constructing the group norms. Some teaching artists develop a contract with the group

---

Sample Norms for Working

1. Everyone has work that must be done outside the studio or rehearsal/performance space.

2. There are times when we will let go of our own preparations in light of new developments.

3. Everyone deserves a place in the circle and is responsible not only for his or her place but the places of everyone else. For example, when we are late or absent or not prepared, we are responsible not only to the teacher but to the entire group.

4. Each individual investigates in what ways one is responsible for the reactions one may have to the mysterious, the unfamiliar, the prejudice, the other.

5. Nobody can *make* me do or feel anything without my own participation.

Figure 3–2. Sample Norms for Working

wherein each individual's signature signifies his or her willingness to take on the responsibility not only for his or her own success but also for that of the group. Some organizations also require parents' signatures and help to promote the connection between the student and his or her family to the work. I like to write the norms on a large sheet of paper and post them in the room whenever we work. That way, we can all see them and refer to them at any time in the process. I also like to leave blank space on the paper, so that we can add or delete throughout. This indicates that the norms are negotiable and are dynamic and evolving, just like the work we generate together.

Although building community always begins a project, it also continues throughout the sessions that follow. The starting and ending rituals are repeated, and exercises such as Chase, and Stop and Go (see Appendix A) become warm-up games for reminding the group that we are working as a community of players with a group identity as well as our individual talents and identities.

Skills Building

Improvisation is fundamental to the skills building process. Some basic rules for improvisation are important to the success of the playing. Most important is the rule that every idea is acceptable as long as it stays true to the character and the situation. Accepting ideas can be a major sticking point for beginning improvisers. Often this occurs because we feel the need to create conflict immediately instead of allowing the conflict to arise from the situation and/or relationships. Key to successful improvisation is to affirm and accept any offer of an idea initially and see what happens from there. All improvisers and teachers of improvisation begin by working on what is referred to as "accepting offers." To begin, students can work in pairs. One student makes an offer, something simple such as "let's go to the beach," and the other accepts and says, "yes!" Alternatively, one student makes an offer and the other blocks and says, "no!" This simple yet elegant exercise quickly reveals to the players how saying "yes" creates possibility for action and saying "no" stops it. As the group continues, the desire to accept offers outweighs the desire to block. It is, quite simply, more fun. Accepting offers also means that we accept the conditions the characters and situations impose on the scene. Staying true to the character and/or situation means that the dramatic action of a scene arises not from conflict but from what happens to the characters as a result of the conflicts that come from the situation.

Once students are familiar with the basic rules for improvising, I introduce CROW (character, relationship, objective, and where). The skills we want to build are our ability to use CROW in whatever situations we create for our improvisations. All of CROW is expressed through action. Our ultimate goal in performance is to present CROW. Actors portray characters through specific behaviors as they interact in relationship with other characters and the setting and are motivated by the desires, needs, and problems of those characters. The elements of CROW are the tools we explore to actively construct the whole. Adding too much information all at once can make the improvisation unwieldy and confusing. Throughout the skills building exercises, I focus students on one element at a time to generate ideas that will be developed more fully in rehearsal. Initially, improvisations are best kept short, lasting only long enough to experiment with the idea, character, or situation. The purpose during the improvisation stage is not to create the whole piece but rather to generate lots of ideas. Allowing for short, multiple explorations of ideas also creates a pulse for the work. It keeps the group actively moving forward during the sessions.

I use the personal inventory of skills and storytelling explored earlier to capitalize on what students already bring to the work. If an individual can juggle, what kind of character might one create who juggles? Easy answers might be a clown, but it could also be a harried mother keeping up with her children. What settings might that character be in? Again, a circus will probably come to mind but it could also be something as ordinary as a post office. How does this character relate to other people? If in a circus, others might be fellow circus performers and audience. If in more ordinary settings, such as a post office, interesting possibilities arise when someone enters juggling packages. The key is to challenge students to use their known skills to construct characters in a variety of settings based on what they bring to the work and develop new skills through improvisation.

Discussions and Selection of Theme or Topic

Because my purpose is to work on skills and improvisation with a goal for performance, the selection of topic or content needs to occur early in the process. From the beginning, this does several things: It sets the expectations for performance; it builds ownership of the ideas for exploration; it signals that the devising process is open to discussion and depends on everyone's contributions; and it sparks decisions that fuel independent research and exploration outside of class time. As Andy Kempe (2000) reminds us, "trusting in the students' ability to generate something from nothing, and perhaps more importantly, encouraging the group to trust in this ability, is pivotal to the devising process" (68).

In many situations, the teaching artist, in partnership with classroom teachers or fellow teaching artists and as a result of the educational purposes of the organization, has already selected the content for the work. In other situations, the selection of the topic and content must come from the group to stay true to the intent of the work. In the latter case, the selection and exploration of the content is seen as an integral part of the whole process and occurs within the process itself. In either case, the goal is to encourage participants to discover whether they, collectively, have enough passion and excitement to sustain them throughout the project. If the topic has resonance with the group, "the enthusiasm and creativity generated by putting on a show can add a dynamic sense of purpose to a group and can foster productive discussions about important issues" (Weigler 2001, 31). When the social and/or educational intentions of the performance will include consideration of the interests and concerns of the specific audience, it might be helpful to identify the intended audience at this point in the process. However, most often, the identification of an appropriate audience arises from the context surrounding the work rather than being the foundation for selecting content. In schools, the audience usually includes parents and peers. In theatres, the audience includes parents, peers, and the general public who attend theatre.

Even when content is preselected by the teaching artist, there is room to make something unique to the group from the content. Remembering that the root of the theatrical experience is story, I begin by tapping into stories. Through storytelling we build connections to the topic at hand or generate possible ideas for the group selection of a topic. By sharing our stories with one another, we express ideas and keep ourselves open to other stories, other perspectives, and ideas with which we are less familiar. We become members of what Barton and Booth call a "story tribe" (1990, 11). The theatre-teaching artist might invite participants to tell stories based on the content. This can be facilitated through journal writing and through improvisations based on our own stories.

Ways of Talking About Our Work

Before moving into exercises that generate ideas and material for performance, we need to discuss and agree on a structure for talking about the work we do together. I provide guidance, but it is important for the group to keep asking questions and generating ideas rather than giving opinions or criticisms. The group needs to suspend judgment to allow for multiple possibilities to emerge. Once rehearsal begins, the performance objective reemerges, and the necessity and deadlines inherent in the performance process dictate that final decisions concerning design, staging, and casting must be made. I, as the director, will make decisions in order to craft a final piece for performance. The degree such decisions can be made through group consensus is partly determined by the context and the time line for the overall project.

Liz Lerman's critical response process, as described by Sheila Kerrigan (2001), provides a helpful structure for those times when the group gathers to discuss the improvised work members have shared during the process. She begins the process with affirmations, asking for descriptions of what stood out, what provoked an emotional response, what seemed true to the situation or problem of the exercise. Challenging students to avoid the generic "I loved it!" response encourages them to use thick descriptions of what they see, hear, feel, and think. This builds vocabulary and critical thinking skills necessary for participating in theatre. The second step encourages the performers to ask questions of those watching the work. Performers ask specific questions that address the intent of the work and the performance. Inviting the performers to ask questions first validates the performers' work and allows them to stay in control of their creation. After (or sometimes during) the performers' questions, respondents can ask neutral questions, such as "what did you have in mind when you . . ." without expressing opinions or suggestions. At this point, if the performers want to go back and work on the idea some more, they do so. If they are willing to receive suggestions, they can ask for that. Or they may decide to put the work aside and perhaps revisit it again in either the improvisation or rehearsal stage. What is important at this point is that the decision rests with the performers. If the performers ask for suggestions, they retain the right to disagree. The final step is always to go back to work. If time allows, it is best to give the performers one more try before either abandoning the idea or moving on to another exercise. I like to write out the steps on a large piece of paper and keep it posted in the room so we can remind ourselves during our discussions.

Improvisations to Generate Ideas/Material

By applying improvisation exercises to the content for devising, the group generates material for performance and deepens their understanding of the content. Michael Wright (1997) refers to the improvisational stage as learning to "work theatrically" (15). Here also is the place where I can stay open to the ideas generated by the group. Usually I have a specific topic in mind. My task is to make the idea visible and transparent and build commitment and interest by creating improvisations for exploration. Throughout the improvisation stage, we record (with either pen or camera) the ideas generated through the work. In my work, I usually construct the play script based on the work done by the group (Nicholson, 2000). At other times, I enlist the aid of a playwright, to create a working script, which is then revised based on the improvisations during rehearsal. Whatever the method and degree of collaboration when organizing material for performance, I involve the participants in recording what happens through the improvisational process. As Andy Kempe reminds us, "endowing students with strategies to record the different stages of the devising process can help students acquire the particularly difficult skill of editing and shaping their work" (2000, 72).

As we improvise to generate ideas and material, I encourage students to use CROW as inspirations for ideas. I create situations based on particular individuals that illuminate the topic or theme. Or I might consider a physical objective and setting for action (building a wall, opening a door, etc.) set in a particular place connected to the theme. I consider a variety of forms with improvisations to help generate ideas. Some examples of possible forms are (1) student-created narratives; (2) found texts, such as scenes from plays, essays, short stories, to play with individually through monologue or with others through dialogue; (3) silent actions or tableaux (frozen pictures) that convey aspects of CROW; and (4) verse or rhythms with or without words. The use of outside resources expands understanding of the content while also generating material for performance. I collect artifacts that connect to the content and encourage students to bring in artifacts such as pieces of text, photographs, paintings, songs, and props. When working in schools, familiar resources such as textbooks, maps, trade books, and pictures become resources for improvisations around the content. This is a time when students are often motivated to conduct outside research as they see how artifacts can energize their improvisations.

Rehearsal/Performance

As the group moves into the rehearsal stage, questions of how to shape the script ideas drive the basic direction of the work. Whereas the improvisation stage depends on the suspension of judgments concerning performance, now the process shifts into decisions concerning the selection of material from what was generated, the order and shape of the work, the casting of roles, and the organization of the space. At this point, I take on a greater role, organizing the working script, and setting the script onto the stage. However, if the group has followed the critical response process and notes have been taken on who generated what material, the particulars of the staging choices that were made, as well as the content of the improvisations, then many of the decisions concerning staging have already occurred. As noted earlier, the time line and content for the project often determine the degree of participation in decisions for rehearsal. What is important to me is to keep the spaces open for discussion and contributions from the participants as much as possible.

In organizing materials for performance, my first step is to review the material generated either through student-created improvisations or improvisations with found texts, artifacts, or other resources. Spreading all of the material out across the floor allows the group to assess visually what has been generated. Although the overarching content or theme will provide the central unifying element, applying the "what stands out" type of questions used for individual pieces to the material as a whole might reveal a piece of music, a prop, a character or group of characters, or a visual image that occurs and reoccurs across pieces. Revisiting the intended audience and, in the case of issue-based performances, the intended messages the group wishes to convey is also appropriate at this point.

The next step is crafting the order of the material. As Michael Wright points out, "the audience usually needs to know certain things first, second, and third for some kind of coherency" (1997, 145). Basic climactic play structure, exposition, rising action, climax, falling action/denouement, and resolution might inform decisions in terms of organizing the whole and making the most of the dramatic potential within each piece. However, as Gerald Chapman reminds us, "no play (no good play) in history has ever followed this pattern slavishly" (1990, 84). Sometimes the linear structure suggested by the basic play structure fits the material and the process best. In other situations, the structure does not present a single story but rather becomes what Kempe calls a "dramatic collage" (2000, 67). Here the material is more episodic and the individual pieces relate to the content in different ways. The topic or content usually suggests the structure for organization.

Discussions surrounding the order and shape of the performance usually lead to discussions and decisions on the organization of space for rehearsal and performance. Again, the content itself may provide clues for the organization of space. Consideration of the actual performance space available will also influence the organization and design of the space. When working in schools, often the performance space is located within a multipurpose room or cafeteria. It might be an actual stage or just an open space. When working in theatres, we have the luxury of a working stage, where the space is designed for performance. For myself, I find it difficult to organize material without having some design of the setting for the performance within whatever space is available. Making sure certain students can be seen and heard often takes priority in how the space is organized. I want the setting to support the young actors so they can successfully communicate to the audience the ideas and material they have worked so hard to bring to performance.

Setting the performance on the stage usually requires that I take on a stage manager/director role at some point. Here, I rely on my practical experiences as an artist to inform the choices I make during the rehearsal process. I am responsible for creating the rehearsal schedule that makes effective use of time and actors, and managing props and costumes and the installation of the set. As the director, I use the ideas generated through the improvisations within the individual pieces and creating transitions to weave the pieces together into a coherent whole. Throughout the rehearsal process, I keep in mind my educational goals whereby everyone participates and has a voice in the decision-making process while moving toward the goal of performance. Reviewing the inventories of skills of students may reveal students skilled in design, organization, or other backstage roles. I strive to find ways to keep everyone onstage and involved in the scenes, either as audience within the world of the performance or as actors within the scene. This keeps offstage time to a minimum and increases the investment of everyone in the whole performance.

As rehearsals move closer to performance, it is important to make time for envisioning possible problems and working together to discuss possible solutions. Forgetting lines, losing props, standing in the wrong place, having the set fall apart are all potential disasters. We give voice to our fears and devise recovery strategies to help each other out. To feel successful about the performance, everyone needs to feel that we are all in it together, and together we will all succeed. Asking students to design a program for their performance also builds ownership and anticipation for the upcoming performance.

Public performance conveys to the audience and the students that I take seriously the ideas and processes they have been engaged in. It is serious work and joyously fun. It is nerve wracking and usually characterized by last-minute rehearsals. Many are the times when I have been rehearsing some final detail thirty minutes before the house opens. Ultimately performance belongs to the actors, and when we work in educational contexts, it is a celebration of work accomplished.

A few practical organizational considerations help me make the most of the performance experience for the group. I make sure there is time and space for the group to warm up together, working in a circle and reminding themselves of the community they are part of. Warm-ups provide a space for getting the jitters out and focusing attention to the work at hand, rather than on the people in the audience. I arrange for volunteers or others to manage aspects in the front of house, such as handing out programs, directing the audience to their seats, and so on so I can spend time with the cast and attend to any last-minute details or emergencies.

Some practical considerations for audiences are also important. Although the audience is often comprised of parents and family members with intimate connections to individual actors onstage, I ask that they do not take pictures or videos during the performance. This follows practice in professional theatre and casts the parents and family in the genuine role as audience members first, doting admirers second. I arrange with the cast that time for pictures will follow the performance and communicate this to parents and audience members. If possible, I arrange for a video recording that can be copied and distributed to students after the performance.

Finally, I encourage students to hold a postperformance discussion with the audience. I set the routine for getting into place for the discussion at the same time we set the curtain call. I give spectators who do not wish to stay a few moments in between the curtain call and the discussion to leave. I ask the cast to sit at the front of the stage and encourage them to select someone to moderate the discussion. Sometimes I act as the moderator. I ask students to introduce themselves and then prompt audience members to ask questions. The goal of the postperformance discussion is not to give thanks, or flowers, or any of those kinds of ceremonies we sometimes see at the end of school performances. The goal is to make visible the process the students engaged in and provide an opportunity for students to reflect on their work and share their reflections with the audience. Once the discussion is ended, I try to carve out a moment for the group to return to the warm-up circle and debrief together on the performance experience. It is important to make sure that the group has at least a moment to share experiences, acknowledge each other, and say goodbye. And then I make certain that another time has been scheduled for final reflections and assessment.

Reflecting

As an actor, I know if I evaluate or judge my work too early in rehearsal I will cut myself off from investigating all the possible choices that are available to me. As a director, I know I must suspend judgments to allow time for actors and designers to experiment and explore. When I apply my artistry to teaching, I understand that assessment of the process and product is critical to the success of the project. For young students, and even seasoned professionals, untangling judgment of the self from judgment of the performance is difficult and takes time and care.

Judgments of quality are familiar to the artist. As an actor, I am judged every time I audition for a role and every time I step on stage. My individual performance and the entire production is scrutinized by other artists, the public, and critics. And those judgments directly affect my success as a working artist. The criteria I use and the criteria others use to discern what is good in the theatre are often highly subjective and controversial, and yet, in conversations about our work, invariably a group of actors and directors will find places of agreement. In the professional theatre, the performance is the focus for evaluation. How the artist got to the product is rarely evaluated, except in ways that are reflected in the performance.

When I apply my artistry to teaching, my focus shifts to understanding student progress and development and building students' knowledge and skills thinking about, performing in, and responding to theatre. Having students keep notebooks or processfolios encourages them to record the work accomplished throughout the project and respond to the overall development of the project rather than on the final performance. Examples of items to include in processfolios are in Appendix B. Developing a critical eye for one's own work takes practice and responsive guidance. Complementary to the processfolio, I sometimes engage students in individual conference sessions and students can participate in peer assessments as either partners or small groups, using their processfolios as the basis for discussion. In such sessions, students and teaching artist talk about what processes, methods, tools, and abilities are learned, and what is valuable in terms of the agreed-upon goals of the project. The processfolio encourages "individual students to employ a range of devises for recording, visually, aurally and through notation, what is being created, allows the teacher to monitor and report on elements of each individual's contribution to and understanding" of such things as information and the value of background research; the different forms of expression and how those forms are generated; the structure and sequence possibilities; evaluation of their own and others' contributions; and the audience response (Kempe 2000, 74).

The measurement of student performance is another way to assess student progress. A number of options exist for measuring performance. Three of the most commonly used in the arts are checklists, rating scales, and rubrics. Checklists, written lists of performance criteria, are most often used to diagnose progress. As the individual's performance is observed, the scorer determines whether the criteria are present in the performance. Rubrics are designed to provide descriptive of different levels of performance within each criterion. The different levels might be labeled as excellent, good, fair, or poor or can be assigned a number (i.e., 4 = excellent, etc.). Within each criterion, the rubric describes the demonstrated behaviors indicating excellent, good, fair, and poor. Rubrics are especially useful in providing more detailed feedback and discriminating levels that move beyond the present/not present of the checklist rating scale. Examples of performance measurements are in Appendix B.

When scoring or rating performance, the critical step is to define the criteria on which the numerical system is based. The particular knowledge and skill objectives for the given exercise inform the development of criteria; however, in keeping with the constructivist approach to learning, asking students to help develop the criteria on which they will be evaluated builds group commitment to the work and makes visible for everyone what they are working on in any given performance evaluation. Asking students to score or rate themselves and others disrupts the familiar teacher-driven power structure in evaluation and distributes the responsibility for judging progress among all members of the group.

Developing the criteria through class discussion and asking everyone to contribute to the scoring process also helps to develop the critical eye. Individual performances based on the techniques and principles within the individual exercise are rated or scored through close observation and clear definitions of criteria. Multiple performance assessments are necessary in order to create a fair and complete evaluation of student progress and abilities. Setting aside time for formal evaluation of performance throughout a project provides students and the teaching artist with feedback on their progress. Numerical measurements can be used for grading or other evaluation purposes.

In program evaluation, the goal is to provide evidence of both individual progress and achievement and a normative picture of the group development within the project. Normative evaluations compare students with each other. If measurement is critical to overall program development, then it is important to design performance tasks and methods for scoring that are valid, reliable, and focused. To ensure validity, the task and the criteria must match at least some of the goals of the program. To ensure reliability, individuals doing the scoring must agree on the criteria and the degrees to which it is seen in the evidence. Using the same task and rubric at the beginning and at the end, having the same teaching artist throughout the project, and making certain that all students receive the same instruction control for some of the variables that could skew results.

In today's climate of accountability, there is a great deal more emphasis on assessment and evaluation of students, teaching artists, and programs than when I began working in schools and with professional theatres. Processfolios and performance assessments provide helpful evidence for reflecting and beginning the cycle anew. However, I believe it is also important to remember, as Michael Wright (1997) does, that "theatre itself is a game: it has rules, true, but within those parameters the essence is fun" (24). As we work hard, we also play hard. "The play's the thing," Shakespeare has told us. As a theatre-teaching artist interested in teaching performance, I want to keep my eye on the joy of performance while at the same time focus on the fun of getting to that place.

In the Year of the Immigrant

Theatre-Teaching Artists in an Elementary School

The project described in this chapter illustrates how theatre-teaching artists in elementary schools work alongside classroom teachers to create projects that make instrumental use of their artistry in order to explore other areas of content within the daily school curriculum. In America's elementary schools, immigration in the history of the United States is most often studied in the fifth grade. Two fifth-grade teachers, a reading specialist, a music specialist, and three teaching artists (two in theatre, one in music) formed a partnership to create a project that resulted in a theatrical production performed by approximately sixty fifth-grade students. Set in a public urban elementary school, the project called on the curricular area of social studies for the content of the musical theatre performance.

Preparing the Project

The project began with meetings between the teaching artists and the school staff. The reading specialist in the school envisioned a multidisciplinary theatre project that would include all of the fifth-grade students in the school. We began our initial meetings by discussing the curriculum and the experiences of the students. Students in the school reflected the diversity of the surrounding community and the influx of

Asian immigrants to the area throughout the 1980s. Families from Cambodia, Laos, Vietnam, and Thailand who had recently immigrated to the Pacific Northwest meant that many students in the school had firsthand experiences with immigration. Other students had grandparents and other relatives who had made the journey to the United States in the past. The teachers wanted to include the students' personal experiences in the study of immigration while also looking at the history of immigration in the United States. The reading specialist wanted to use the personal experiences as a way to encourage English learning, in both reading and writing. Together, we decided that if students were encouraged to speak, write, and read about their own experiences in relationship with reading and writing about immigration in general, we might increase motivation and interest in the overall topic.

The reading specialist and teaching artists wrote a grant to the local arts commission. In the project description, we outlined the goals for the project as threefold: (1) We wanted to provide teachers and students with experiences in theatre that related to the specific area of immigration within the fifth-grade curriculum; (2) we wanted to empower the students by including their own voices and stories in the work we did; and (3) we hoped to guide the students to creating a successful musical theatre performance for peers and parents. Once funding was secured for the project, we set out to draft a plan and create the schedule.

Our plan included both our work with students while we were at the school and the teachers' plans for classroom study. The teachers planned to use the classroom textbook as a way to construct a time line for the history of immigration in the United States. They also wanted to show a film on Ellis Island to introduce students to that particular place and time in immigration history. In addition, they planned to have all students read Betty Bao Lord's book, *In the Year of the Boar and Jackie Robinson* (1984), a historical novel that chronicles the journey of a Chinese family who immigrates to the United States in 1947. As told through the eyes of a young girl, the book is very accessible to fifth-grade students and highlights many of the challenges young people face when entering a new school, a new community, and a new country. The teachers thought this book would help inspire students to tell their own stories and at the same time encourage the reading skills in English many of the students needed to practice. Finally, the teachers planned to ask the students to interview family members and present oral and written family stories of immigration.

As we discussed the teachers' plans, we devised activities that we felt would take advantage of what students were learning in the classroom by structuring creative writing activities and theatre improvisations around the family stories, the content presented in the textbook, and the literature. The music teaching artist, Joseph Seserko, decided to compose original songs, based on students' improvisations and ideas, and work with the music specialist to teach the songs to the students. Our overall goal for the theatre and music was to allow students to express their individual experiences within the community of the school while at the same time express their membership in the larger community of citizens of the United States. Working with the teachers, we decided to divide the project into three main areas that reflected the immigrant experience: leaving/departure, journey/transition, and arrival/accommodation (see Figure 4–1).

Time and space are always issues when working in elementary schools. Flexibility is key for all participants, and we were fortunate to have a school staff that supported the idea of the project and teachers who were willing to change daily schedules to accommodate the theatre work. The project took place in the middle of the school year, which meant the students were familiar with one another and with general classroom routines and expected behaviors. Students were already familiar with basic music skills and some had participated in after-school drama activities outside of school. It was decided that the teaching artists would work with the students three days a week for six weeks. The two fifth-grade classes of approximately thirty students each would meet separately for the first five weeks, and then all of the students would come together for final rehearsals for the performance during the sixth week. Joseph, the music teaching artist, worked with the music teacher during fifth-grade scheduled music class in the music room once a week until the final week of rehearsal. The school was structured in open classroom style "pods," which meant the two classrooms were open to one another. Although the teachers were able to teach each class separately within the open arrangement most of the time, we knew that it would be difficult to have theatre activities going on in one area of the pod without disrupting the other group trying to work on classroom activities. The teachers arranged for us to meet either in the multipurpose room or in other pods while those classes were at recess or on field trips. The classroom teachers attended all of the theatre sessions and took notes on what the students were doing. The principal arranged for our exclusive use of the multipurpose room during the sixth week so we could create the performance space and rehearse. The physical education teacher agreed to have his classes meet outside or in the fifth-grade classrooms during that week.

Teaching Artists	**Classroom Teachers**
Introduce the project through community building and basic theatre skills.	Introduce topic through interview assignment with family members.
	Organization of individual student journals.
Leaving/Departure	**Leaving/Departure**
▪ Packing improvisation.	▪ Create a time line of various groups leaving different places to come to the United States.
▪ Creative writing: Moving away from and coming to.	
▪ Song composition on "Moving."	▪ Read In the Year of the Boar and Jackie Robinson.
▪ Rehearse scripted scenes from In the Year of the Boar and Jackie Robinson.	
Journey/Transition	**Journey/Transition**
▪ Transportation tableaux.	▪ Use textbook to investigate different modes of transportation.
▪ Creative writing: Letters from America.	▪ Watch film on Ellis Island.
▪ Rhythm poem compositions.	▪ Continue reading In the Year of the Boar and Jackie Robinson.
Arrival/Accommodation	**Arrival/Accommodation**
▪ Welcome improvisations.	▪ Finish reading In the year of the Boar and Jackie Robinson.
▪ "Carl" song composition.	
▪ Rehearse scripted scenes from In the Year of the Boar and Jackie Robinson.	▪ Field trip to the United States Immigration Office, Port of Seattle.
▪ Creative writing: What do we love about the United States?	▪ Prepare and present oral reports on interviews with family members.
▪ Creative writing: I'm proud to be….	▪ Finish written reports on interviews.
▪ Final song composition.	
Rehearsal	**Rehearsal**
▪ Create the blocking and staging.	▪ Compilation of individual student notebooks.
▪ Props, set, and sound arrangements.	
▪ Practice!	▪ Test on historical dates.
Performance	**Performance**
▪ Coordination with teachers, students, and parents for final celebration.	▪ Organization of final performance times.
	▪ Student reflections on performance.
▪ Post-performance discussion with groups.	▪ Collection of notebooks.

Figure 4–1. Teaching Artists' and Classroom Teachers' Project Plans

Teaching

Theatre-teaching artist Gretchen Orsland and I planned and taught the theatre lessons, wrote the script, and directed the final production. Most of the time we taught the students together. Because we were working artists at the time, we sometimes had to trade off teaching times to allow for our own audition and/or rehearsal schedules. Each week, the three of us (including Joseph, the music-teaching artist) would meet to read over student work and compose the pieces for what would become the final script. Joseph would share the songs he had composed, and we would discuss production elements such as props, set, and sound. We also met with the teachers and specialists once a week to discuss the project and to hear about what was happening in the classrooms. The teachers also helped to organize student notebooks in which each kept his or her notes and handouts from classroom study and the writings generated during the theatre work. The notebooks were collected each week to track student progress throughout the project and provided inspiration for the final script.

The project occurred during the winter term of the school year. Because all of the students knew one another and were familiar with classroom expectations in terms of behavior, we used introductions and community building exercises as a way for us to get to know the students and to reinforce the discipline needed for working together on a theatre project. Given the large number of students in each class and the relatively short time to develop the project, we knew we would have to begin work on the project right away. Basic acting skills were developed within the specific exercises; and as we progressed, we introduced theatre vocabulary, such as *CROW*, and staging terms, such as *upstage* or *stage right*, in the context of working on the improvisations and scripted scenes. Our challenge was to devise exercises that would generate material while at the same time introduce students to the theatre art form. The limitations of time and the numbers of students meant that we sometimes had to skip extended discussions about the work with the students. This is a perennial challenge for the theatre-teaching artist working in schools when performance is an ultimate goal; however, by meeting regularly with the classroom teachers, we knew they were reinforcing and discussing the work throughout the week and felt comfortable that students were given opportunities to talk about the process.

To generate material and ideas for the performance, we combined time for improvisations with time for creative writing. When working on improvisations, often the whole group would work at the same time to maximize participation. With thirty students in a class, it was difficult to share every improvisation with each other. Allowing time for writing ensured that all of the students had an opportunity to express their ideas in their notebooks. We selected words and movements from the writing and improvisations to create the final scenes for performance. Gretchen and I adapted the scenes from *In the Year of the Boar and Jackie Robinson* to create play scripts. We divided these scenes between the two classes to provide an opportunity for each class to work on part of the book. Joseph taught his composed songs to both classes, knowing that everyone would be singing in the final performance.

We adapted general theatre exercises to create improvisations around the central theme of immigration. Throughout history, people, as a result of force or choice, have pulled up roots and made extremely hazardous journeys to find a new home. For this project, we wanted to create improvisations in which students could explore the emotional and sensory experience of the personal struggles and revelations people encounter as they make these journeys and express those experiences through character and situation. The three stages of the immigrant journey—leaving/departure, journey/transition, arrival/accommodation—gave us a structure for organizing the improvisations. The situations and categories mirrored what students were studying in the classroom. This helped us integrate our theatre work with the work of the classroom teachers. Joseph also used the three stages as a way to organize the songs he had composed for the performance. A complete running order with selections from the final script and lyrics from the songs are in Appendix C.

Leaving/Departure

Leaving/departure marks the beginning of the immigrant experience. It is also something that most of us have encountered at some point. We suspected that students would be familiar at the very least with moving, either from one home to another, from one classroom or school or neighborhood, going on a trip to a friend's house overnight, or traveling with family on a longer journey. The first activity focused on packing a bag in anticipation of a journey. We created improvisations that used the action of packing and then introduced a series of characters and motivations for the action of packing that led students to imagine the immigrant experience. Students worked individually and pantomimed the actions of packing their things. We encouraged students to commit to the situation, letting their characters' emotions inform the way they performed the actions. The situations we presented began with familiar experiences, such as packing to visit a friend who lives in another city. Mirroring the classroom study on immigrants traveling to Ellis Island from Europe, we asked students to imagine they had just been told that their family would be moving to the United States. They would travel on a ship for many days and could take only one container for their things. Another mirrored the situation in the book *In the Year of the Boar and Jackie Robinson*. Students imagined receiving a letter from their father telling them that it was now time to join him in America. A final situation was created to honor the experiences of many of the students' parents and some of the students themselves who had spent time in refugee camps before coming to America. In this situation, students imagined that they would have to leave their houses quickly and could take only a few things because they might have to swim or walk a long distance in order to escape.

After each situation, we discussed their characters and the emotions they felt. We also asked students to write descriptions in their note-books. The prompts for writing included ideas expressed during discussion, observations we made during the work, and specific choices individual students made, such as what they chose to put their things in (i.e., a suitcase, a box, a paper bag, etc.) and what they decided to pack (i.e., clothes, a stuffed animal, a photograph, etc.).

When we leave a place, we take not only our physical belongings but also our memories. Our second activity was a creative writing exercise that built on the pantomimed experiences and descriptions the students had written. We asked students to think about the various situations and the characters they chose for themselves as they were packing to leave. We asked students to make two columns side by side on a piece of paper. On one side, they wrote the words *away from* and on the other, *coming to*. We modeled this on a large piece of paper so students could see what we had in mind. We also encouraged students to raise their hands if they had trouble writing so we could help them. Our goal was to generate lots of ideas and not worry about spelling at this point in the writing. We reviewed each situation, asking students to complete the sentences on both sides of the paper, visualizing the character they had in mind and both the home place they were leaving and the imagined place they were going to. To encourage descriptive images, we prompted the students with questions such as what does the place look like? Are there colors? Are there trees? Plants? Water? Big buildings? What is the weather like? Is there a smell or taste to the place? A special food or plant? Is it a rough place or smooth? What do you hear in this place? Birds? Cars? People? What else? Is it an angry place, a sad place, a place full of fear or happiness? After writing, we invited students to share one or two of their sentences with each other. In the performance, all of the students took places on stage and started pantomiming packing. They could choose which situation they wanted to use. Once the actions were begun, students spoke selected sentences, based on the collective writings, to accompany the packing (see Appendix C).

For our final activity in the leaving/departure section, Gretchen and I adapted two scenes from *In the Year of the Boar and Jackie Robinson*. We cast and rehearsed one scene with each group. In the first scene, Bandit's grandmother informs her that her father has sent for her and her mother. They are going to leave for America. We divided lines from the text, expressing the fears and concerns among members of the class, and they whispered the lines to Bandit (Lord 1984, 13–4). In the second scene Bandit asks her grandfather for a new name. Again, members of her family look on as she tells her grandfather, "since I am going to America, I would like an American name." The grandfather agrees and asks her if she has any suggestions. Bandit decides on Shirley Temple, a popular actress of the 1940s. The crowd waits for the answer. Grandfather agrees and officially names her Shirley Temple Wong (Lord 1984, 17–19).

In the music classes, Joseph used the word *moving* to compose the beginning of a song. Repeating the word over and over, he introduced students to the rhythm he had in mind. Then he asked students to make lists of intangible things people brought with them: traditions, languages, and hopes they imagined immigrants had brought with them, such as better schools or jobs. Using the students' lists, he brainstormed words that would rhyme with each other, such as *education* and *occupation,* and composed the song "Moving" (see Appendix C).

Journey/Transition

The journey of the immigrant marked the middle part of our teaching. We knew students would be watching a film about the journey of European immigrants who landed at Ellis Island in the early part of the twentieth century, and they would be reading about Shirley's journey from China to California and then by train from California to New York City in the late 1940s. We wanted to also include more recent journeys of immigrants by airplane, landing in places such as Los Angeles and Seattle, as well as the hazardous journeys by foot and small boats from places such as Mexico and Cuba. Our goal for this section was to explore the physical representations of such journeys and the emotions people registered when arriving in a new place. We also wanted students to investigate what might seem new or foreign to others about the United States.

The improvisation we created for this section was a series of tableaux based on different modes of transportation. We introduced the skills needed for the improvisation by playing the games Snap and Click, and Triangles (see Appendix A). We used descriptions from the classroom textbooks to construct a list of the various types of transportation immigrants throughout history have used to make their journeys and constructed a list of possible choices (wagon, horse, car, foot, bus, plane, boat, etc.). The students worked in groups of five, choosing a mode of transport and creating a tableau of a group traveling in that manner. Once each group had created an initial tableau, we asked the groups to begin moving in the rhythm of the mode of transportation and to add sounds to their movements that matched the form. We then asked students to create another tableau showing their arrival in the place matching the mode of transportation (an airport, a border crossing, a harbor). Each group shared its tableaux, beginning with the first tableau, moving in rhythm, and ending with arrival.

After sharing tableaux, we asked students to write letters from their perspective of someone who lives in America to someone who is just coming. We began by asking students to brainstorm what makes the United States different from other countries. What do they think is particularly impressive, interesting, fun, fearful, or odd? Once we had a list of ideas, we asked the students to decide whom they might write to—a brother or sister, a grandparent, or a best friend—and let the age and relationship inform what they would choose to tell them. Working individually, each student wrote a letter in his or her notebook. Most of the students chose to write to a friend. We collected these letters and created one letter to a friend by combining the ideas of the students.

In performance, we divided the stage into three areas. In one area, we asked two groups from one class of students who had created tableaux of ships coming into harbor to perform their actions while two students read a selected description of seeing Ellis Island (see Appendix C). In a second area of the stage, we had a group of students create a tableau that matched Shirley's description of her train trip across the country. Two students read the words from the book: "As the wheels of the train clacked along the tracks, they seem to chant four more days, just four more days. Three days, just three days. Only two, only two, only two. Tomorrow, tomorrow. Today!" (Lord 1984, 24). In the third area, center stage, we arranged three groups of students who had devised more contemporary tableaux of transportation to perform those while three individual students read our created letter.

In music class, Joseph brainstormed with students a list of things they most enjoyed in their classrooms, homes, and neighborhoods in the United States. He then composed a rap-style song that used items from the list, which the students performed as a spoken choral piece. The final piece included these. As Joseph was working with the students on this composition, they discovered their lists also included many different kinds of food that exemplified the diversity of our country. Joseph composed a "food march" that incorporated many of these items and became a spoken choral piece for the production (see Appendix C).

Arrival/Accommodation

The third section of the project focused on the arrival and the subsequent accommodation that immigrants face after they arrive. In the classroom, students read about immigrants arriving at Ellis Island and the questions immigrants were asked. They also discussed the process for becoming a citizen and what kinds of information newcomers would need to learn in order to pass a citizenship test. In the theatre work, we wanted students to explore both sides of the experience, as one entering the country and one already here. We also wanted students to investigate how it feels to be someone new and the ways others can make that difficult or easy. Finally, we wanted students to celebrate things they enjoyed in the United States, while recognizing the difficulties of today's world.

First, we created a list of questions for newcomers, based on the questions students had studied in the classroom and ones they thought were important. The questions ranged from official questions, such as the number of people in their family and their reasons for coming to the United States, to more personal questions, such as how much money they had and if they had any diseases. Working in pairs, the students practiced saying the questions to one another in rapid succession. One student asked the questions quickly without allowing time for the other to answer. Then they switched roles. After the exercise, we discussed how difficult it was to think fast and how immigrants might feel when facing such a list of questions. In performance, we used selected questions shouted out at one another (see Appendix C).

We thought it was important to counter the question-asking improvisation with another perspective in which immigrants were appreciated and students could express what they most wanted for new people (and themselves perhaps) arriving in the United States. We created another improvisation whereby the students worked in pairs to welcome newcomers to our country and give them gifts to start their new lives. Again working in pairs, the students imagined a door between them. One student walked up to an imaginary door and knocked. The other opened the door, said, "Welcome," and gave the person a gift. As they gave the gifts, we encouraged students to say what it was. Then the students switched roles so each could give gifts to the other. After the improvisations, we asked the pairs to write down the gifts they gave to one another. We collected their ideas and created a scene using the students' ideas. In performance, the students stood in a line across the stage with their backs to the audience. A knocking sound was heard. One by one they turned around, opened the imaginary door, and spoke their lines out to the audience (see Appendix C).

In music class, Joseph asked students to imagine a person their age just coming to the United States and entering school. He asked them to list the kinds of things the new student might do or wear that would make him seem different. They discussed how the other students might treat the new student in the beginning. Using their ideas, Joseph wrote the song "Carl," but didn't finish the ending. After teaching it to the class, he asked the students to think about how the students in the song treated the new student and how that might make that student feel. Together they created an ending for the song that showed a way for the students to accept the new students into their school (see Appendix C).

We adapted two more scenes from *In the Year of the Boar and Jackie Robinson*. One class rehearsed a scene in which Shirley encounters her schoolmates playing baseball on the playground. Shirley is enlisted to play and quite by accident she steals home. The class cheers and calls her Jackie Robinson, referring to the great baseball player who, in the same year as the book's setting, made history by becoming the first black man to play professional baseball and by perfecting the art of stealing home to score a run (Lord 1984, 76–82). The other class acted out a scene in which Shirley asks the teacher why the kids called her Jackie Robinson. We asked one of the classroom teachers to play the part of Mrs. Rappaport, the teacher. In the book, Mrs. Rappaport explains to Shirley why Jackie Robinson is a national hero and why he personifies what is great about our country by saying:

> Baseball is not just another sport. America is not just another country. In our national pastime, each player is a member of a team, but when he comes to bat, he stands alone. In the life of our nation, each man is a citizen of the United States, but he has a right to pursue his own happiness. (Lord 1984, 92)

We knew that immigration is a perennial issue in the United States and that many families still struggled to accommodate to their new country. Although many of the scenes and improvisations we created led students to a place of acceptance of newcomers, we also wanted to recognize the challenges that everyone continues to face. Joseph composed a song that we felt gave voice to these issues without diminishing the positive aspects of the other pieces. The title was "This Country's Getting Crowded" (see Appendix C).

We also wanted to honor the student's own experiences and interviews with family members the students had done during their classroom study. We asked the students to write short monologues based on their interviews that began with sentence, "I'm proud to be a(n) _____ American." In the blank, they were to write their ethnic heritage, such as a Chinese American, an Irish American. We prompted them to write something that they felt was unique about their family living in America. We collected these and selected several to be read in the performance.

Rehearsal/Performance

Throughout the weeks of classes, in both theatre and music, we collected the student writings, the adapted scenes,and Joseph's songs. Our task was to weave them all together and organize sixty students on the stage for performance. During the final week, all of the students met together in the multipurpose room. Thanks to the principal, we secured risers that gave height to the back of the stage and provided a more interesting playing space. We divided the stage into three main playing areas: downstage center and upstage right and left. Because of the number of students, we decided that all props would be pantomimed and that costumes would be white T-shirts and dark pants with multicolored ties around the waist. The ties could be removed to become scarves tied around the head, shawls around the shoulders, or welcoming signs waved in the air. The teachers became doubly important at this time, helping to organize class groups and keep rehearsals from erupting into chaos.

Gretchen and I decided that rather than following the linear outline of the stages of immigration we used for the teaching, we would mix it up a bit to make the piece more interesting and provocative. We began the performance with the song, "This Country's Getting Crowded" and used it as a reprise at the end to highlight the fact that immigration is a contemporary issue for all communities and worthy of the time spent investigating the experiences of people across time. We knew we also wanted to celebrate the diversity of the student population and provide a message that such diversity is one of America's greatest strengths. We placed the student-written monologues at the end before the reprise.

Once we had the running order, rehearsals concentrated on casting the scenes to make certain that everyone had speaking parts in at least one scene and creating the blocking so that students could move from place to place on the stage efficiently and effectively. All sixty of the students remained onstage throughout the whole piece, sometimes sitting on the sides as audience members while others performed a scene. Everyone sang all of the songs. We knew we didn't have the time or the expertise to create dances so we used simple marches and groupings to create a sense of movement without choreography. Most of the individual scene work had been set during teaching time, so students stayed in their class groups as a management technique. Having a classroom teacher play Mrs. Rappaport proved to work out not only to make the character believable but also to provide an authority figure onstage during rehearsal and performance.

At the end of the performance, all of the students formed a large circle, untying the sashes around their waists and tying them together to form a giant circle of connected fabric. This task was, without a doubt, the most technically difficult, and I'm not sure any of us believed they would actually accomplish it in performance. Like so many of the miracles of theatre, they did and it created a wonderful visual effect for the final reading of the personal monologues. The circle broke apart during the reprise of "This Country's Getting Crowded," and the students formed two chorus lines across the stage so they were in place for the curtain call at the end of the performance.

Reflecting

We were asked to do this project three times at the school over the course of three years. Each year, the exercises remained the same, with different words and actions created by the different groups of students. The songs remained the same. The project ended when two of the teachers retired and we, as the teaching artists, went off to pursue other projects and interests. Looking back now, I am struck by several key ingredients that I believe made the project a success and several key items that I see now were sorely missing.

A key element for success was the extraordinary collaboration between the school community and the teaching artists. The fifth-grade teachers and the reading and music specialists devoted precious instructional time to the theatre activities and took on active roles as teaching assistants and even actors in the work. The parents supported the project by providing matching funds for the teaching artists and production costs. They attended the performances and even organized a potluck supper for the participants and the audience at the end. The administrative staff made copies of scripts and sent out announcements to families about the performance. The principal made certain we had the support we needed and invited district personnel and other outside partners to attend the performances.

Another key ingredient was the constant communication between the teachers and the teaching artists. This resulted in a tight connection between the content studied in the classroom and the content explored in the theatre and music work. One of the challenges for teaching artists working in elementary schools is to integrate curriculum content in authentic and meaningful ways. As outsiders, we are not always privy to the scope and sequence of the curriculum, the resources and information the teachers use on a daily basis, and the skills they are teaching. The textbooks, curriculum ideas, classroom assignments, and learning targets were clearly communicated to us throughout the planning stage. During teaching, we checked in weekly with each other to make sure our schedules were in sync with one another. The teachers helped the students collect their writing assignments into individual journals so they would have a record of what each had accomplished while we blended the individual ideas together to form one cohesive script.

Missing from the project was a close assessment of individual journals and incorporation of other strategies for providing evidence of student learning. We did not collect data on what students actually learned about theatre or immigration, nor did we use pre- or posttest type measures. We did not compile the scores on classroom tests. The teachers provided anecdotal information indicating that students did well and that interest in the project was high. The fact the project was renewed and funded for three years gives some evidence that it was seen as contributing significantly to the school and to learning; however, if this project were done today, all of us involved would be much more attuned to the need to collect strong evidence of student learning. We might use strategies to measure what students know at the beginning and end of the project; we could document student experiences by recording not only their written work but also their attitudes about the work; we might keep track of student attendance to see whether the project had a positive effect on students' motivation to come to school; we could video record the theatre work and the final performance in order to have a better record of what actually occurred. One of the problems with these kinds of projects is that there is no final script that would make much sense to an outside reader. This is true for this project. What we are left with is a list of activities, scrawled on yellow notebook paper, a running order, the songs, some sample collections of words and scenes, and a recollection of performance.

Fortunately, a social studies education professor at the University of Washington attended one of the performances and wrote an article about the project. Writing for his column in *Educational Leadership*, Dr. Walter Parker wrote that "along with democracy and economic development, the gathering of diverse peoples in the United States is one of the most important ideas treated in the social studies curriculum," but he wondered whether fifth-grade students could work with the topic in a way that would help them "build a reasonable, albeit initial, understanding." After viewing a performance of *In the Year of the Immigrant* and talking with the teachers and parents after the performance, Dr. Parker concluded that the collaboration between teachers and teaching artists had indeed resulted in such a display of understanding and "the performing arts met the social studies, and the rendezvous worked splendidly." Dr. Parker noted that while many of the students in the school were bused, some spending two hours a day traveling to and from school, "none missed any of the performances." Quoting one of the parents after the performance, Parker wrote, "something like this is enough to make you think it's all working" (Parker 1989, 84).

5   Play Ball

Theatre-Teaching Artists in a Professional Theatre for Young Audiences

The Seattle Children's Theatre (SCT) is one of the largest professional theatres for young audiences in the United States. The theatre's mission is to provide professional theatre and theatre education experiences for children with affordable daytime matinees for schools, public performances, and classes. Each year the theatre strives to present artistic, thematic, and appropriate productions for families. The theatre employs Equity actors and often commissions professional playwrights to create new work for its seasons of plays. In November 2004, SCT was recognized by *Time* magazine as one of the top five children's theatres in the country.

The SCT Drama School offers a range of after-school and Saturday classes throughout the school year. During the summer months, the drama school operates a large program with classes for preschoolers through young adults. A hallmark favorite at SCT Drama School is the Summer Season of student productions, featuring fully produced plays directed by teaching artists and performed by young people from fourth grade through high school.

When the Seattle Children's Theatre became an independent nonprofit theatre in the early 1980s, it had a small education program that featured some after-school, Saturday, and summer classes for children ages six through eighteen. During this time, I worked as the education director and one of the resident teaching artists. In 1983, the theatre began the Summerstage program in response to the desire for performance experiences for dedicated young performers, ages nine to fifteen. The program provided students who had completed basic acting classes at SCT or had experience in theatre from other places to focus on concentrated study in rehearsal techniques, character development, and ensemble acting. Students auditioned for admission into the Summerstage program and were expected to approach the Summerstage experience as a serious (yet fun!) endeavor. Our original vision for the Summerstage productions was to create, produce, and perform quality productions on the main stage of the theatre during the summer months as a complement to the professional theatre productions offered during the school year. The student performances were free and open to the public. Our expectations for the quality of acting, directing, and production were high. We hired designers to create sets, costumes, props, and lights and theatre-teaching artists to teach and direct the productions. Over the years, the Summerstage program proved to be very popular. Today, Summerstage, now titled the Summer Season, produces eight student productions during July and August. Subscriptions as well as single tickets are sold for the Summer Season and the performances provide box office revenue to support the education program of SCT. I believe the ongoing success of the program is due to those original high expectations and the quality work of the theatre-teaching artists and students from the beginning.

Preparing the Project

Education programs set within professional theatres obviously focus on the art form. For young children, classes focus on theatre exploration. Basic acting classes, special-interest classes (i.e., musical theatre, stage combat, and Shakespeare), and performance/production classes are usually offered for students ages eight to eighteen. Some theatres, such as SCT, also offer intensive actor training institute programs for advanced high school and college age students who are interested in pursuing careers as performers. Whatever the class or the level, professional theatre education programs foster a love of the art form that will inspire future generations to continue to see and/or create theatre throughout their lifetimes. The goal is to introduce students to the world of theatre through active participation in the making of theatre. Unlike teaching in elementary school programs, the teaching artist in the professional theatre education setting focuses primarily on teaching theatrical skills and vocabulary and applying those in performance. Like any theatrical endeavor, the work might relate to many disciplines beyond the theatre; however, the learning objectives for the programs are usually to learn acting skills, script development, rehearsal and performance disciplines, and techniques. When a teaching artist is hired to teach for a professional theatre program, he or she usually meets with the education staff to determine the specific guidelines and curriculum for the class he or she is to teach. Sometimes a teaching artist might propose a specific class to the theatre. The degree to which the teaching artist determines the curriculum of a given class or program depends on the size of the theatre's educational programs, the overall goals of the program, and often the relationship between the teaching artist and the theatre's education and artistic staff.

As education director for SCT and part of the year-round educational staff, I was involved in the development of the curriculum for all the classes and for the Summerstage program in particular. As a small theatre education program, the three members of the education staff also served as teaching artists. We taught the basic acting classes during the school year and created programs as our student population grew. We began the Summerstage program to serve the needs of those students who had already taken the basic acting classes and were ready for more intensive experiences in performance. Students were required to have taken at least one other acting class or had other acting experiences and to audition for the Summerstage program. Auditions were held in the spring so students and families could make summer plans around the performance schedules, and we could prepare the programs to meet the needs of the particular groups of students.

Like most professional arts education schools, our goal was to keep the class size small in order to provide maximum interaction with the artists for every student. However, also like most arts education programs, we depended on tuition to cover much of the costs of the program. Our compromise was to set class size for the Summerstage performance classes at between fifteen and twenty students. As teaching artists, like theatre teachers in middle and high schools, finding quality scripts with interesting and significant roles for fifteen to twenty actors was and continues to be a primary challenge. In addition, we wanted the Summerstage program to complement and expand the student experiences in theatre. We wanted to find or create scripts students might not have encountered in a public school theatre program. We also wanted to find scripts that were age-appropriate but intellectually and artistically challenging. One solution was often to create new scripts, based on a theme or adapt a script from literature. Unlike devising, wherein the group or the teaching artist creates the script during the rehearsal process, the Summerstage program relied on scripts created by the teaching artist before the program began. This was due in part to the four-week time frame of the summer program. It was important for designers to have the script before classes began. In addition, the student goals for the program focused on teaching the skills and techniques needed for an actor to rehearse and perform a play successfully. A detailed outline of a working script on the first day of classes allowed us more time to meet those goals.

As a teaching artist for the Summerstage program, I created scripts that were more dramatic collage than linear stories. The project *Play Ball* grew out of my desire to create a script that would have multiple opportunities for students to play a variety of roles and the fact that my favorite sport is baseball. I love the structure of the game: nine players on two teams, the rules of play, the fact it is not played against a clock. I like the aesthetic ordering of the space: the diamond shape of the infield, the green grass of the outfield contrasted with the dirt of the base paths, the house design of home plate, the dugouts, the bleachers. I also love the stories of baseball: Lou Gehrig's heroic speech at Yankee Stadium; Jackie Robinson breaking the color line; the little leaguer who practices every evening with his dad. I approached Gretchen Orsland, my long-time teaching artist partner, with the idea of creating a script using baseball as the theme and two groups of Summerstage students as the actors.

Both of us were teaching one Summerstage class. Gretchen's group had sixteen students and mine had seventeen. Together we had a total of eight boys. We knew that if we wanted to do a play about baseball, we had to find material that would challenge and interest the girls as much as—if not more than—than the boys. All of the students would need to display some of the athletic skills of baseball players (i.e., throwing a ball, swinging a bat, miming a catch) just as any actor would need to if he or she were playing a character in sports. We decided to keep the classes separate and divide the script between the two groups. That way, both of us would have time to teach acting skills and rehearsal techniques with our smaller-sized group. Only in the final week before performance would the two groups come together for rehearsals.

To prepare the script, we began researching the topic of baseball, looking for plays, novels, short stories, and poems that featured baseball. As our research expanded, we were delighted to find that so many artists—writers, painters, playwrights, and musicians—found baseball as interesting as we did. Because we were creating a performance for educational purposes and would not be charging admission to the performance, we felt we could adapt and borrow from a number of sources to create a performance collage on the topic of baseball that would provide all of the students with significant roles to play and challenge each one to develop strong acting and musical theatre skills.

We adapted selections from W. P. Kinsella's novels *Shoeless Joe* (1982) and *The Iowa Baseball Confederacy* (1986) as monologues. The opening scene in Act One from Neil Simon's *Brighton Beach Memoirs* (1984), featuring a young Eugene playing a pretend game of baseball on his front porch, also seemed appropriate and would challenge one of our young actors. Ernest Thayer's classic poem "Casey at the Bat" (1967) provided an opportunity for an ensemble choral piece. *Diamonds Are Forever: Artists and Writers on Baseball* (Gordon 1987), published by the Smithsonian Institution's Traveling Exhibition Services and New York State Museum in Albany, features a collection of short poems, essays, and stories along with paintings of players, baseball fields, and artifacts. We adapted many of the poems and essays, to provide scenes and parts for a wide range of student actors, girls and boys. Obvious music choices always sung at baseball games included "Take Me Out to the Ballgame" and "The Star-Spangled Banner." The song "There Is No Team Like the Best Team," from the musical *You're a Good Man, Charlie Brown* by Clark Gesner (1967) offered an age-appropriate number, with accessible and fun characters and challenging music.

The musical *Diamonds*, an off-Broadway musical presented by the Baseball Project Company in 1984 and published by Samuel French in 1986, provided additional numbers for large groups. "Let's Play Ball," written by Gerald Alessandrini, features a chorus-line-type song, appropriate for the whole group of students. Scene 13, "Stay in Your Own Backyard," written by John Weidman, Lynn Udall, Karl Kennett, and Pam Drews, tells the story of the Negro Leagues and the integration of African Americans, such as Jackie Robinson, to the major leagues. A gospel number, "He Threw Out the Ball," written by Larry Grossman and Ellen Fitzhugh, offered another chorus number with challenging singing parts. We also included the song "Ka-razy," written by Doug Katsaros and David Zippel, featuring a group of fanatical fans at a baseball game. The final number, "Diamonds Are Forever," written by John Kander and Fred Ebb, provided a strong ending for our performance collage about baseball.

As we collected, adapted, and arranged the material into a working script, we also left spaces for students to create scenes of their own. We knew the success of the performance would come from a committed investment in the play by the students. We would need to win that commitment by honestly giving them a voice in as many decisions surrounding the script as we could manage. Gretchen and I agreed we needed to provide opportunities for students to build ownership into our script by writing and performing some of the own material, generated through improvisations during rehearsals.

Our classes met for three hours Monday through Friday for four weeks. Gretchen's class met in the mornings and mine in the afternoon. Both of our classes met in the theatre so we worked on the stage or divided up into smaller groups and worked in the other areas backstage and in the house. Unlike a school setting, the students did not know one another. Some of them had taken acting classes at SCT and some had been students of ours in those classes. But much like the first day of rehearsals in a professional theatre setting, the group itself was new. We planned to devote the first four days of classes to community building activities and skills building exercises so each group could get to know one another and we could assess the skills and interests of the individual students. Throughout the first week, we planned to present the topic of the play to the students through improvisations based on baseball. We were prepared that some of the students would be less than excited about the sport but felt confident in the variety of material and opportunities to learn music and choreography in addition to acting. Because our play included many musical numbers, we hired a musical theatre director to teach the music, accompany the performance on the piano, and choreograph the musical numbers.

After the first week, Gretchen and I planned to divide the script between the two classes and cast the parts based on student skills and interests. During weeks two and three, our plan focused on the rehearsal of the selected scenes, monologues, musical numbers, as well as improvisations to create student-devised scenes. We planned to begin each class with group warm-ups and theatre games. The music director/choreographer alternated days, working with my class one day, Gretchen's the other, throughout the three weeks of class time. When the day included music and/or dancing, students did a vocal and dance warm-up. The music director would choreograph the company numbers with each class. He put them together during the final week. Other numbers were divided between the two groups. On days without music, half of the class time would be spent on blocking and rehearsing the scripted scenes and monologues. If students were not in a scene being worked on onstage, they would be expected to practice their scenes on their own. The other half of the session was spent on large group scenes and improvisations. Twenty to thirty minutes at the end of each class session was to be devoted to reviewing the work done that day, discussion, and reflection. During the final week of classes, both classes met together for an extended day so we could put the pieces together and prepare for performance (see Figure 5–1).

Teaching

Narrative text and poems are difficult for any actor but especially for young actors just learning their craft. They are not written, as plays are, with actors in mind. In narrative text, the writer often leaves the interpretation up to the reader. In interpreting such texts for the stage, the actor (and director) has to find a character and a relationship within a situation that is dramatically interesting in order to make the transition successfully from page to stage. Gretchen and I knew that this would be a challenge for the students so we adapted the narrative pieces into dramatic scripts ahead of time. For example, I adapted the poem "Casey at the Bat" by creating a cast of characters that included two narrators, the players on the field, the players waiting in the dugout or batting (one of whom is Casey), and the fans in the stands. I divided the lines of the poem between the two narrators and staged it according to the action indicated in the poem. In another instance, Gretchen adapted a selection of an essay by Roger Angell, by creating the characters of two scientists. As they spoke, they measured and took apart baseballs to provide action for the narrative text.

> It weighs just over five ounces and measures between 2.86 and 2.94 inches in diameter. It is made of a composition-cork nucleus encased in two thin layers of rubber, one black and one red, surrounded by 121 yards of tightly wrapped blue-gray wool yarn, 45 yards of white wool yarn, 53 more yards of fine cotton yarn, a coat of rubber cement, and a cowhide (formerly horse-hair) exterior, which is held together with 216 slightly raised red cotton stitches. (Angell, quoted in Gordon 1987, 32)

Other pieces of narrative featured a particular player or action of a player, which provided the character for the actor to play. For example, in the poem "The Base Stealer," the actor interpreting the text played the part of the player on base and getting ready to steal. The action was created by the situation and added to the dramatic effect of the words.

Week One: Morning and Afternoon Classes Working Separately

Monday	Tuesday	Wednesday	Thursday	Friday
Community Building	Community Building	Community Building	Community Building	Community Building
Skills Building	Skills Building	Skills Building	Skills Building	Skills Building
Music and Choreography or Improvisations on Baseball	Music and Choreography or Improvisations on Baseball	Music and Choreography or Improvisations on Baseball	Music and Choreography or Improvisations on Baseball	Music and Choreography or Improvisations on Baseball
Discussion and Reflection	Discussion and Reflection	Discussion and Reflection	Discussion and Reflection	Discussion and Reflection

*Dividing of script and casting occurs after Week One.

Weeks Two and Three: Morning and Afternoon Classes Working Separately

Monday	Tuesday	Wednesday	Thursday	Friday
Warm-Ups	Warm-Ups	Warm-Ups	Warm-Ups	Warm-Ups
Skills Building (dance, singing, or acting)	Skills Building (dance, singing, or acting)	Skills Building (dance, singing, or acting)	Skills Building (dance, singing, or acting)	Skills Building (dance, singing, or acting)
Music and Choreography or Rehearsals and Improvisations	Music and Choreography or Rehearsals and Improvisations	Music and Choreography or Rehearsals and Improvisations	Music and Choreography or Rehearsals and Improvisations	Music and Choreography or Rehearsals and Improvisations
Discussion and Reflection Warm Ups	Discussion and Reflection Warm Ups	Discussion and Reflection Warm Ups	Discussion and Reflection Warm Ups	Discussion and Reflection Warm Ups

Week Four: Whole-Day Rehearsals with Both Groups

Monday	Tuesday	Wednesday	Thursday	Friday
Warm-Ups	Warm-Ups	Warm-Ups	Warm-Ups	Warm-Ups
Rehearsals	Rehearsals	Rehearsals	Rehearsals	Dress Rehearsal
Lunch Break	Lunch Break	Lunch Break	Lunch Break	Discussion and Reflection
Rehearsal	Rehearsal	Rehearsal	Dress Rehearsal	Evening Performance
Discussion and Reflection	Discussion and Reflection	Discussion and Reflection	Discussion and Reflection	

Figure 5–1. Teaching Plan for Play Ball

Poised between going on and back, pulled
Both ways taut like a tightrope-walker,
Fingertips pointing the opposites,
Now bouncing tiptoe like a dropped ball
Or a kid skipping rope, come on, come on,
Running a scattering of steps sidewise,
How he teeters, skitters, tingles, teases,
Taunts them, hover like an ecstatic bird,
He's only flirting, crowd him, crowd him,
Delicate, delicate, delicate, delicate—now!
(Robert Francis, quoted in Gordon 1987, 122)

In keeping with our plan, we created improvisations to devise original scenes to add to the scripted text. The students created characters in various situations either to complement the scripted material or to come up with new scenes. We brought in baseball artifacts (i.e., baseballs, bats, hats, gloves, trading cards, pennants, scorecards). In one scene, a group of students used pennants and scorecards as props. They created individual characters who were rival fans at a baseball game. This became a complement scene for the "Ka-razy" song. In another instance, two girls used baseballs as inspiration for two monologues, wherein each took on the persona of a baseball. One girl improvised her story as an autographed baseball, sitting alone on the shelf, telling how once the initial excitement had worn off, she felt neglected and forgotten. The other told hers as a worn-out baseball, tattered and dirty, stuck into the bottom of a backpack, taken out every day and hurled across the grass or knocked silly by a wooden bat. In performance, the girls wore oversized white sweatshirts and rolled out into the playing area side by side and shared their stories with each other.

Gretchen and I encouraged the girls in our classes to tap into some of their initial disappointment over doing a play about baseball through improvisation. We prompted them to think about everything they hated about baseball. We then encouraged them to think of things they might like about the sport. The girls created dueling scenes wherein one group discussed how much they hated hot dogs, the hat hair of brothers wearing baseball caps all summer long, and how confusing it was to watch a baseball game with all of the rules and signals and breaks between pitches, and another group discussed the cute uniforms the players wear, their cravings for hot dogs and peanuts, and the thrill of a home run. These were scripted and included in the performance.

Rehearsal/Performance

We used the baseball structure of two teams who play the game in innings. One team bats in the top half of an inning, the other in the bottom half. We organized the script according to the inning structure. The team up to bat was onstage while the other team sat either in the dugout or in the bleachers. This idea fueled the set design. The stage became a miniature baseball diamond with bleachers upstage center, the pitching mound center stage with the bases appropriately configured around the mound, home plate downstage center in line with the mound, and the dugouts just off the stage downstage front. A flagpole was situated upstage right and a makeshift scoreboard was upstage left.

The structure of the game also gave us the structure of the show. During the last week, when both groups rehearsed together, we referred to our individual classes as teams. We began the play as if we were beginning a baseball game. Some students from my team played characters who worked in baseball stadiums, hawking programs at the door as the audience came in and handing out real bags of popcorn and peanuts. Some students from Gretchen's team entered the stage as groundskeepers, laying out the baselines on the field and setting the bases. Nine students from each class entered the stage and stretched and took practice swings as players do before the game. Once the audience was in their seats, the players and workers exited and gathered backstage. An announcer from the sound booth introduced the lineup of players. My team lined up on the first base side (stage left) and Gretchen's team on the right base side (stage right). For costumes, the players wore simple baseball-style T-shirts and a baseball cap, and each carried a bat. After the lineup, the teams turned and faced the flag, the audience stood and joined the players in singing the national anthem as an American flag was raised. Then the announcer shouted, "play ball," and the cast performed the opening number, "Let's Play Ball." After that, my team took their places in the dugout and Gretchen's team performed the first scene. Throughout the rest of the piece, the teams would rotate with one in the dugout and the other on stage, except when both teams performed in a musical number. When appropriate, students took positions on the bleachers as fans at a game; however, most of the time, the audience was cast as the spectators. Because there is no halftime in baseball, we created a rain delay so we could take a break between acts one and two. While neither team won or lost, the play ended the way it had begun. After the final musical number, the teams exited the stage and the lights dimmed. Individual students returned to the stage in pairs or in small groups picking up props, sweeping the bleachers, and erasing the lines on the field. Once all of the students had entered, the students shared lines we adapted from two essays on baseball. The first was taken from Thomas Boswell's "How Life Imitates the World Series":

> Doubtless there are better places to spend summer days, summer nights, than in ballparks. Doubtless. Nevertheless, decades after a person has stopped collecting bubble-gun cards, he can still discover himself collecting ballparks. And not just the stadiums, but their surrounding neighborhoods, their smells, their special season and moods. (Boswell, quoted in Gordon 1987, 13)

The second was adapted from A. Barlett Giamatti's "The Green Fields of the Mind":

> It is designed to break your heart. The game begins in the spring, when everything else begins again, and it blossoms in the summer, filling the afternoons and evenings, and then, as soon as the chill rains come, it stops and leaves you to face the fall alone. (Giamatti, quoted in Gordon 1987, 142)

Reflecting

After the performance, one girl told me that she did not like baseball and was originally quite disappointed that she would have to work on a baseball play for four weeks. Even though her personal feelings about baseball had not changed, she was glad that she stuck it out and even admitted that she had learned a great deal about the sport. More importantly, she also said she had learned a great deal about acting: how hard you had to work physically, how difficult it was to sing and dance at the same time, how creating a character and finding the right emotion in a scene was thrilling and scary. She admired all of her fellow actors as she watched them work onstage.

This was our goal for the Summerstage experience. And this anecdotal comment, remembered by me years later, seems to prove that our goals were met. Throughout the project, Gretchen and I did a great deal of informal assessment, discussing what students were learning to do, which students needed more help, which students could use the challenge of creating a scene for the play. We both kept notebooks on the project, and I have used those in writing this narrative of the project. Although we encouraged students to keep their own notebooks, we did not collect them. Our focus was on the development of the student skills in performance, rather than on assessment of student learning. This is a challenge for the theatre-teaching artist who engages in the creation of a performance with young people. Preparing for the assessment of a project needs to occur during the preparation of the overall project. Looking back now, I see places for assessment. We could provide vocabulary lists and a list of the skills required within the games. We could ask students to respond to specific prompts for reflecting on the work at the end of every week. We could ask students what they found surprising. Like a baseball player watching tapes of games just played, we could videotape the rehearsals and review them during class time.

Gretchen and I have talked a great deal about this project. Both of us are struck by how much of what we did during that summer was intuitive and spontaneous and how much we remember. The hours of preparation turned into moment-by-moment teaching decisions and long afternoons of reflection and discussion. Both of us have file folders full of notes from class sessions, scribbles of scenes on yellow notebook paper, and photocopies of the text we selected. I found a copy of the musical *Diamonds*. The memory of that theatre performance, like memories of baseball games watched and played, lives forever in our hearts. And we suspect it does with those students who played ball with us for four weeks one summer fifteen years ago.

6 Boundless

Theatre-Teaching Artists in Community

Theatre-teaching artists often find themselves working for organizations and communities whose missions carry with them social and political agendas. Theatre is instrumentally used to further the social and political missions of the overall organization. Augusto Boal wrote, "Theatre is a form of knowledge; it should and can also be a means of transforming society. Theatre can help us build our future, rather than just waiting for it" (1992, xxxi). When we listen to each other and make meaning of our personal experiences in the context of dramatizing them for others, "we are likely to strain toward conceptions of a better order of things in which there will be no more wars that make women weep. We are likely, in rebellion against such horror, to summon up images of smiling mothers and live and lovely children—'everything we love,' metaphors for what ought to be" (Greene, 1995, p. 123).

Unlike a professional theatre, such as the Seattle Children's Theatre, the Seattle Peace Theatre was a community youth theatre. One of its founding members, Helen Strickland, had worked for the Peace Child Foundation USA, creating productions with international casts of young people from the United States and what was then the Soviet Union. Helen brought together community activists, who had worked with her on peace projects for many years through such organizations as Educators for Social Responsibility, Doctors Without Borders, and Plowshares, and theatre/music artists, who had worked with her on

Peace Child to create the Seattle Peace Theatre in 1989. The mission of the nonprofit organization was to broaden and strengthen the efforts for peace by creating an environment for young people and artists from different countries to use theatre to communicate and learn more about this important issue from each other. The results would be shared with the public through the creation of theatrical productions to bring the issue of peace to the larger communities.

Building on the successful theatre exchange program of the Peace Child Foundation, Helen, and David Samuelson, a theatre-teaching artist, began by initiating a partnership with a theatre in one of Seattle's sister cities, Tashkent, Uzbekistan. During the summer of 1989, music and theatre-teaching artists and young people gathered together in a small community outside of Seattle to create a theatrical piece titled *Peace Is Possible*. After that initial effort, the theatre reached out to the Young Actor's Musical Theatre in Moscow, Russia, to create another partnership for peace. In the summer of 1991, four teaching artists and sixteen young people between the ages of twelve and eighteen traveled to Moscow to work on a new piece. Political events in the Soviet Union that summer brought a halt to the production. Russian and American artists and young people found themselves in the middle of a failed coup attempt and what eventually became the fall of the Soviet Union. Whereas I had been involved as a volunteer and occasional teaching artist with the theatre since the beginning, I was the lead teaching artist of the American delegation during that summer.

After returning home, the Seattle Peace Theatre invited the Moscow company to bring a group to Seattle the following summer of 1992. At the suggestion of the Russian company's artistic director, Alexander Foyodorov, the theatre also invited Rosmarie Metzenthin and her company of young actors of the Children and Youth Theatre from Zurich, Switzerland, to join the effort. Alexander and Rosmarie had worked on similar partnerships in the past. My experiences working in Moscow in 1991, coupled with the extraordinary global changes that were happening so quickly, fueled my interest in and commitment to the Seattle Peace Theatre.

This work was my introduction to the kind of work many teaching artists engage in when they apply their knowledge and experiences in theatre to social and political concerns of local and/or global communities. I found myself deeply committed to the mission of the theatre and enthusiastically agreed to serve as lead teaching artist for the exchange. Throughout 1991–1992, all of us prepared for a tricountry exchange, with artists and students from three countries, speaking three languages and bringing experiences from three decidedly different cultures. Our goal was to create a production that called on the diverse theatrical expertise and the social, cultural, and political experiences and concerns of the three theatre groups while at the same time addressing the common goal as peacemakers that could be expressed in theatrical form. The result was an original play titled *Boundless: A Musical Across Borders*.

Preparing

A teaching artist working within a community organization often assumes other duties beyond that of preparing and teaching the educational curriculum of the art form. The context of the community organization carries goals and activities that expand the responsibilities and concerns of the individual artist. Most teaching artists join community youth theatres because they are drawn to the educational, political, social, and/or cultural perspectives of the particular organization and its commitment to the conscious empowering of the individuals within the organization. The Seattle Peace Theatre's mission rested on the belief that if theatre-teaching artists and young people have intensive and multiple opportunities to communicate with each other on matters concerning peace, tolerance, and global understanding, all individuals will feel empowered to promote peaceful communication and global understanding in their own lives and countries. This belief was reflected in the structure of the summer exchange programs and the involvement of the teaching artists.

The program was designed as a summer camp where young people and teaching artists, counselors, and other adult volunteers devoted four to six weeks, living together and working together to develop the culminating theatre event. Everyone lived together throughout the rehearsal and development process in a camp-type setting located outside of the host city. While the majority of time was spent on theatrical activities and rehearsal for performance, everyone participated in a variety of outside activities, sharing our different cultural perspectives through games, dances, songs, and recreation. As in any summer camp, young people roomed together and everyone took their meals in a common dining room. The teaching artists were responsible for preparing and teaching the theatrical curriculum including the direction of the final production but were also expected to participate in the day-to-day living together. In addition, counselors and other adult volunteers from each country were responsible for supervising the young people outside of organized class time. Many also participated in the performance process, helping with props, costumes, sets, and stage management duties. For performances, the group moved into the host city. The visiting teaching artists, counselors, adults, and young people stayed with families throughout the community. In most instances, the young people stayed with their fellow company members from the host country, and the visiting teaching artists stayed with their fellow teaching artists. Other adults stayed with board members and volunteers of the host organization. Clearly, the teaching artist's involvement with the Seattle Peace Theatre included much more time and commitment than when teaching in schools or in a professional theatre's educational drama program.

In 1992, our company was comprised of fifty-four young people ages twelve to nineteen: seventeen Swiss, fifteen Russian, and twenty-two American. There were eight teaching artists from the three companies. The American teaching artists took the primary lead in most of the activities as they were most familiar with the language and had the most time to prepare. Three theatre-teaching artists from the respective countries collaborated on teaching acting and improvisation, and directing the final production. Four music-teaching artists, one American and three Russian, taught singing classes, and two of these artists composed the music for the production. A Swiss dance-teaching artist taught movement classes and choreographed the production. The Seattle Peace Theatre hired an American professional playwright to write the play and the American music-teaching artist acted as conductor. Five American counselors were also hired, and the Swiss and Russian companies each brought three to five other adults to act as counselors and production assistants.

Needless to say, language was a challenge throughout the exchange. Our theatre hired two interpreters (German and Russian) to help with language. The Russian company brought an English translator as well. Most of the Russian young people and artists spoke limited English and German. The Americans spoke little or no Russian and German. In addition to German, most of the Swiss spoke English quite well and some Russian. We trusted that the physical and emotional language of theatre and music would help bridge the gaps and result in a shared language, forged from the experiences during the camp. Because the play would be performed in Seattle, it was agreed that most of the play would be in English. With the help of the interpreters, we also agreed we wanted to include the other languages when it seemed artistically possible.

Preparing for the summer exchange included many administrative and managerial details that the board members and volunteers of the Seattle Peace Theatre had to address. Those who were hired as teaching artists and some of the young people selected to participate also pitched in with many of the organizational elements. Throughout the school year of 1991–1992, we raised funds, secured camp and performance venues, arranged for visas and travel, organized the home stays, and set the overall schedule for the program. Many of the American young people had participated in the 1991 exchange program. They recruited other students to apply. Prior experiences with theatre were not the primary criteria for selection. Rather, we conducted interviews and held workshops on improvisation and creative writing to determine the interest and commitment of those who wished to participate in the summer exchange. Once the twenty-two young people were selected, we held weekly meetings to work on details and develop skills and build community within our American group. Safety was a concern and all of the adults, including teaching artists, took first-aid and CPR classes. Although community norms for participating in the theatre work would be developed with the whole group, it was important to set policies and agreements for physical and emotional safety issues that might arise in the living situations. Policies and contracts were created on these issues, translated, and sent to the others. Although these details demanded a great deal of attention and were important to the overall success of all the exchange programs, my purpose here is to focus on the artistic and educational preparation of the theatre activities and the ultimate performance.

Key to preparing the theatre curriculum was establishing the collaboration between the three lead teaching artists of the three companies. I use the term *teaching artist* but, in actuality, our conceptions of the term varied a bit. Alexander was the artistic director of the Russian youth theatre. His concerns focused on theatrical training in musical theatre skills and the mounting of musical theatre productions. Over the course of our work together in 1991, we had many conversations concerning the differences between training and education and what I embraced as a constructivist approach to creating theatre with young people in service to the larger goals of cultural understanding and peace of our organization. Although he was not opposed to such views and wanted very much for his company to participate in these kinds of experiences, he was most comfortable working with written scripts and a more traditional style of directing, making most of the artistic decisions himself and then telling his company members what to do. Rosmarie, on the other hand, was (and is) a highly recognized theatre educator in Switzerland. She operated her own theatre school for young people ages four to eighteen and was more comfortable with my own educational perspectives and the mission of the Seattle Peace Theatre. She often worked with young people to develop original pieces. Her productions with children were most often based on familiar fairy tales, and productions with adolescent company members often focused on social and political issues.

We communicated throughout the school year by fax and telephone about the scope of our production. Given the short time (four weeks) of the exchange program, the Seattle Peace Theatre engaged a playwright to write a working script prior to the summer, rather than attempt to devise a play during group rehearsals. We all agreed, however, that the playwright would work with the group during the rehearsal process and incorporate ideas from the group into the final performance. Seattle playwright Carl Sander had worked on similar productions for the theatre's earlier exchanges and agreed to work with us on this exchange. Suzanne Grant, the music-teaching artist for the Seattle Peace Theatre, joined our team as the American composer and music director for the production. Carl's working script gave us a structure to organize rehearsals, generate additional material, and make revisions. The program was four weeks in duration: three weeks of rehearsal and a final production week before performances.

The first three weeks were spent in a camp setting outside of Seattle. The final week was spent in rehearsals and performances in Seattle. We worked Monday through Saturday at the camp, and on Sundays we rested and did recreational activities such as hiking and swimming. Curriculum for the international company was organized to meet the needs of the overall mission of the theatre. We worked on community building activities that cut across cultural and language barriers every day. We also wanted to mix up the groups of young people from the different companies. It would be too easy to fall back on working with people one knows and who speak the same language. Each morning everyone assembled for basic physical warm-ups and games that did not require words (see Appendix A). Then the fifty-four students were divided into three mixed groups and participated in three classes every morning. The dance-teaching artist from Switzerland taught a basic movement class. Suzanne and the Russian music-teaching artists taught singing. Alexander, Rosmarie, and I alternated time teaching basic improvisation and acting classes. The groups rotated between the three classes for the reminder of mornings. We continued this schedule throughout the process, although as the performance got closer, the time spent in classes focused more on what was needed for the production rather than general skill building.

I knew, based on my experience and conversations with the other companies, that the theatrical skill (acting, singing, dancing) levels of the Swiss and Russian companies were more developed than those of the Americans. Some of the young people in our theatre studied theatre in school or with other outside organizations, such as Seattle Children's Theatre. However, the Seattle Peace Theatre did not offer classes on a regular basis, nor was it set up to be a theatre school in its own right. I recognized that it would be important for everyone to spend time learning skills together in the morning classes. This would allow time for the teaching artists and young people to get to know each other's strengths and ways of working and help with casting for the production. The morning schedule also allowed Carl time to make revisions to the play based on the afternoon rehearsals (see Figure 6–1). Evenings were spent doing recreational activities and allowed time for the individual students to work on their roles in the production.

Carl based his play on the current political events and issues the world was facing at the time. Once the students were assembled, he added their ideas and concerns as they arose during rehearsals. Many of the young people from Russia, as a result of the dissolution of the Soviet Union, were concerned about meeting basic needs, having enough food to eat, a comfortable home, and a loving family. The adolescents in the Swiss company had worked on a play about the influx of refugees to Switzerland because of the war in Bosnia and the tensions that was causing in their country. The threat of war in other countries and the plight of the refugees loomed large in their minds. In the United States, the young people expressed worries about the threat of AIDS and other diseases and the lack of tolerance for differences they perceived in their own schools and neighborhoods. All of the groups expressed environmental concerns. They wanted clean air and water for the world.

The play was titled *Boundless: A Musical Across Borders*. Carl set the play in an imaginary time and place. The play's narrator finds a diary and reads the story of a past time when people were suffering and seeking escape. Three groups of refugees flee their respective lands in the hopes of finding peace. One group is fleeing disease. Another seeks refuge from war and the third group from intolerance. All are seeking to create a place beyond their perceived boundaries where each group can live in peace with one another and the natural world. The action of the play begins when the three groups converge on the stage, each in the hopes of building a ship they can sail to another place. As they interact and struggle with each other for control of the ship, they discover that leaving will not solve their problems. Rather they realize the future is in their hands. They must

Three Weeks in Camp

8:30–9:00	Warm-Ups
9:00–10:00	Dance, Music, and Acting/Improvisation Classes
10:15–11:15	Dance, Music, and Acting/Improvisation Classes
11:30–12:30	Dance, Music, and Acting/Improvisation Classes
12:30–2:00	Lunch Break
2:00–6:00	Rehearsals
6:00–7:30	Dinner Break
7:30–10:00	Evening Activities

Final Week of Rehearsals

8:30–9:00	Warm-Ups
9:00–12:00	Rehearsals
12:00–1:00	Lunch Break
1:00–6:00	Rehearsals

Figure 6–1. Schedule for Boundless

stay and work together to create what they all want: a family, good health, a home, a peaceful life with tolerance for all, and a pollution-free world.

Teaching

Learning the arts is often referred to as learning the languages of the arts: languages of abstract movement, musical notes, physical gestures of emotions and pantomimed actions of character, lines, and color on a page. Nowhere was this more evident to me in teaching theatre than the work I did for the Seattle Peace Theatre. I cannot speak for the other teaching artists' experiences, but I feel confident in saying that all of us became much more attuned to multiple languages humans use to communicate. Because of our spoken and written language differences, our morning theatre classes focused on teaching these languages so we did not need to rely on words.

The acting and improvisation exercises concentrated on representing action and emotional and physical characteristics through silent gesture and pantomime. We created lists of common relationships: parent–child,

doctor–patient, employee–boss, actor–audience, and so on and pantomimed potential scenes between the two. Objects aided the exercises,
providing concrete centerpieces around which we could center specific
situations and dramatic conflicts. A young man might pick up a rock,
threatening to throw it at a classmate, be seen by the head teacher, stuff
the rock in his pocket, and slink offstage. A young girl might play with a
balloon, finally inflating it after several tries and then skipping off to play.
We set up group conflicts, with two lines facing each other and moving
to a beat, encouraging students to allow the reasons for opposition to
emerge through physical action. We created scenes in which students
began by playing familiar games (jumping rope, bouncing a ball, leapfrog)
and encouraged them to create relationships and situations as they continued to play the game. We always had markers and paper available to
draw pictures as a way to communicate to the partner the setting one had
in mind. These physical skills were important not only in communicating
the characters and actions of the play but also in our day-to-day living
with each other.

Rehearsal/Performance

Afternoon sessions were devoted to rehearsals. It took two days to read
through the working script because of the time to translate. The rest of the
week we decided to generate ideas and material within the respective language groups based on two key elements of the play: the issues presented
in the three groups and the dreams for a safe place to go. Although the
play was written and spoken in English, Carl also encouraged the students to repeat lines in German and Russian to capture the multilingual
nature of the whole group. This was also true of the composers. Suzanne
Grant and Volodia Vladimirov (the Russian music-teaching artist) wrote
the songs in English. Choruses within the songs were translated into
Russian and German and sometimes repeated in the various languages as
well. Speaking English was a challenge for many of the Russian students
especially. We asked the American students to help individual students
with the English. The German and Russian students, in turn, helped the
American students learn to sing the songs in the other languages.

During the second week, we cast the play based on the ideas and
writings of the students. Some students had clearly committed to certain characters and had already begun to develop inner motivations and
thoughts. Others were cast according to skills and experience, relying
on those with more acting or musical skills to play key characters that

scenes required. Instead of like-language groups, the three groups in the play were composed of students from the three countries. We did this as a way to reflect that the issues in the play were global issues and affected everyone regardless of their nationality. Once the play was cast, I directed the play with help from Rosmarie and Alexander.

The second and third weeks of rehearsals during teaching proved exciting, difficult, and sometimes tedious. My directions for each scene had to be translated into two other languages. We were very fortunate to have one translator who spoke all three languages. Throughout the rehearsals, the work would start and stop for translations. The group got accustomed to the start and stop rhythm after a time and there was a great deal of pantomime. All of the adult artists spent the evenings discussing ideas, working on revisions and musical compositions, and planning for the next day. We encouraged the students to use their ideas to fuel their individual characters in each of the young actors. Four young women in the war group cared for a baby and dreamed of worlds without weapons. Those in the ill group dreamed of a place where everyone is cared for. Students in the intolerance group came up with the idea that, rather than fleeing intolerance directed at them, they were fleeing diversity in the search of sameness. They dreamed of places where their possessions were safe from others, where no one might bother them, and where they could live without differences. Students in all of the groups dreamed of places with green mountains, blue skies, and clean water. A few wondered if any such places existed at all.

Two adults from the Russian company served as set designers for the production. They worked with a technical director/carpenter from Seattle. The set was comprised of scaffolding upstage center, connecting to the center stage playing area by stairs to stage left and a ramp on stage right. The play called for a ship or vessel that could be assembled by the actors during the course of the play. During rehearsals, we improvised with found objects to cobble together to form the basic frame of a ship. We brought in pieces of fabric that were tied together to form a sail. The adults built a mast in three pieces so the students could put it together on stage as they built the ship. The students used their own backpacks or made bundles from fabric or scarves. One of the adults in the Swiss company designed costume pieces to identify members of each group and to add color to the plain T-shirts and pants the actors wore. Parents of the Seattle young people worked with the costume designer to construct the costume pieces. A happy discovery was the exchange between the various production artists and adults from the three countries, all working to support the joint production.

Boundless was performed four times over the course of one weekend. The opportunity to perform the play multiple times allowed the young actors to settle in to their parts, relax, and enjoy the work everyone had worked so hard to create. After each performance, we held postplay discussions with the actors. Each group had designated someone to act as its spokesperson during the discussions (the role alternated for each performance) and the translators were on hand to aid in the discussion. As was expected, many of the audience members had questions for the Swiss and the Russians outside of the play. Given the extraordinary nature of the exchange, there were also many questions about the process of creating the play. All of the teaching artists and adults attended every performance. The performances were sold out for the entire weekend. The written script for *Boundless* is included in Appendix D.

In a review for the *Seattle Times*, Misha Berson pointed out that this group was "part of the first generation in half a century to share a world where Russia and the United States are not ideological enemies, where nuclear war does not seem inevitable, and where cultural exchanges between former foes have become almost commonplace" (1992, TEMPO 13). Still, the crossing of international boundaries never comes easy. Our exchange and the ultimate production mirrored the struggles of countries trying to solve problems and coexist together. As Alexander Foyodorov put it, in the beginning, everyone smiles at one another, but then the process of sharing ideas comes and compromises have to be made. If progress is to be gained, agreements must be forged and power must be shared in order to achieve the collective goal. As one song aptly put it, "it's not so easy to find a land of peace."

Reflecting

We collected final evaluation surveys from all of the participants. We also asked the American parents to complete evaluation surveys. We videotaped the performance and took photographs of the process. We selected quotations from the surveys, scenes from the videotape, and photographs in our reports to the various funding agencies that supported the project. Not surprisingly, all of the participants felt they had learned a great deal about each other, most especially the customs and habits of daily living. The American students were impressed with the artistic abilities of the Russian and Swiss young people. During the postplay discussions, audience members were impressed with the way the young people seemed to work together. Some asked the young people if they thought the play would make any difference in terms of the world issues. Most of the students expressed uncertainty but felt that they, as individuals, would at least think more about them.

In 1993, I traveled with the Seattle Peace Theatre to Switzerland, and we repeated the exchange without the Russian company. During 1994 and 1995, the theatre offered summer programs with young people in Seattle, concentrating on individual needs and local issues. In 1995, the theatre closed up shop. The end of the Cold War and the relative peace in the world had caused a kind of laissez-faire attitude toward global exchange and peacemaking that made raising funds more difficult. I sometimes wonder though if our success in bringing people together led to a feeling of false security. Today, the events of September 11, 2001, the Iraq war, the terrorists' acts in Spain and in London suggest there is much more work to be done. Peaceful reconciliation of differing views, cultures, and political powers is a never-ending process.

When I reflect on this project, I am struck by the ephemeral nature of the work. So much of what happened occurred in the moments of recognition that members of such a diverse group, speaking three different languages from three very different cultural, social, and political situations, were standing side by side on stage with an enthusiastic audience as their witness. Ten years later, I met with five of the American young people from the cast of *Boundless* and asked them what they remembered about the experience. Most of them did not remember the play. What they remembered was the magic of the performance, of looking at each other on stage and feeling the energy and commitment of the collective group effort. One student remarked that he didn't think such a moment would ever be repeated in his life. He was glad about that because he didn't think such moments should be repeated. Another student told me she had started working with young people herself in summer theatre camps. She carried with her a sense of what might be possible and was drawn to creating such experiences for others.

I also asked Helen Strickland, the founder of the Seattle Peace Theatre, to reflect on the years of the Seattle Peace Theatre exchanges. In personal communication on the 10th of July, 2001, she told me, that even now, twelve years later, when she meets parents of young people who participated in the Peace Theatre, they pull her aside and tell her how the experience was a turning point in the life of their son or daughter and for the family. Certainly, the support and countless volunteer hours the parents put into the efforts were evidence of their commitment. Helen reminded me that many of the parents signed their children up with the

Seattle Peace Theatre because they had been "peaceniks" themselves when they were young. The American young people we worked with had little reason to struggle for peace and little knowledge of what peace might mean to them. Helen believes that by rehearsing the play, living together, and trying to find ways to communicate with each other, the "depth of their commitment grew through an understanding of what the struggle for peace really means."

The *Boundless* project was complex. It was messy and not at all perfect. I asked Carl Sander, the playwright, to reflect on the experience of writing it with the other teaching artists and young people during that summer of 1992. In an email to me on the 20th of May, 2001, he wrote:

In judging success and failure of an artistic endeavor it's always difficult to discern between the success of an artistic work to achieve its goal and whether or not that goal is a desirable one in the first place. Then, after the fact, the process can be looked back upon as to whether or not rehearsal time was well used, or the director communicated well with the actors. With the Seattle Peace Theater the process was the goal. We believed that the world would be a better place if young people got together and created art. Creating a piece of musical theater in four weeks is insanely difficult under the best of circumstances. So what we did was throw everyone together in a room with a next to impossible task and see what came out of it. I can think of no better way for people to get to know one another fast. It's as if we created an artificial catastrophe . . . let's get everyone on a boat, sink it and see if they can figure out how to get to shore. It'll break the ice.

7 Looking Toward the Future

In the previous chapters, I have attempted to build a conceptualization of artistry that drives the central activities of the teaching artist's work. I have called on my own practice and my knowledge of others' practice to give examples within those central activities that might illuminate and illustrate how artistry informs the decisions we make in preparing, teaching, and reflecting. As noted in the beginning chapters, arts education, inside and outside of schools, relies more and more on teaching artists to provide guidance and instruction. Because of this, teaching artists are beginning to see themselves as members of a particular profession separate from their profession as artists and emerging members of the larger profession of teachers. Efforts to describe our profession are underway across the country.

John Goodlad, in his study of teacher education in 1990, puts forth the conditions necessary for an occupation to become a profession. The field must have

> a reasonable coherent body of necessary knowledge and skills; a considerable measure of professional control over admissions (to the profession) and of autonomy with respect to determining the relevant knowledge, skills and norms; a degree of homogeneity in groups of [candidates] with respect to expectations and curricula; and rather clear borders demarcating qualified from the unqualified, legitimate programs of preparation from shoddy and entrepreneurial, and fads from innovation grounded in theory and research. (70–71).

He uses these conditions as a way to assess how teacher education programs are doing in terms of meeting these conditions, acknowledging that many of these conditions are largely lacking. "Even today, teaching remains the not-quite profession" (71).

Goodlad's study was conducted in the 1980s. Since then, tremendous strides have been made not only to define curricular standards for students in schools but also to define standards for teachers. Most states require students to pass tests on content and pedagogical knowledge as part of their requirements for certification to teach in public schools. Many teacher educators participate in the creation of those standards and methods of assessment, and teacher education curriculum is often aligned with state academic learning standards. Many programs in higher education have set rigorous entrance requirements for teacher candidates. Still, the needs of supply and demand and the current political pressures make it difficult for members within the field of teaching to build consensus on issues of curriculum, to achieve autonomy in making those decisions for themselves, and to set clear borders on who is adequately prepared to enter the profession. One can imagine that if teachers in general participate in an ill-defined profession, then teaching artists also participate in a not-quite profession.

In the past, just about any artist could label him- or herself as a teaching artist and enter the field. My own journey began in similar fashion. I learned by doing, reflecting on my successes and failures, and building a repertoire of practice over time. I improvised my teaching while I taught young people to improvise in theatre. Learning to teach by teaching is consistently seen as one of the primary ways teachers acquire pedagogical knowledge and skills (Grossman 1990; Lortie 1975). We learn what works and what does not work through experience. We share our experiences with others and learn more methods for teaching. We closely observe our own teachers through a process Lortie (1975) described as our apprenticeship of observation and apply (or avoid) what we saw to our own teaching.

Learning from experience and the numerous hours during our apprenticeships of observation as students provide us with a memory bank for teaching specific content as well as ways for conducting class sessions with young people. There are, however, several pitfalls in relying on our memory banks alone to prepare us for teaching. For one, our memories of teaching come from our own single experience and are not necessarily representative of all students and teachers. They do not prepare us to consider the multiple perspectives, the diversity of knowledge and experience that is the reality of our world. They limit our conceptions of how students learn and teachers teach to a narrow band of possibilities. Second, our memories restrict the possibilities within our content area, our art form because of the selections made by our teachers and ourselves. And third, our memories do little to help us understand the goals and thinking/feeling, the subtext if you will, that drive the actions of our own and others' teaching. Clearly, if we are to take seriously our artistry in teaching, we need more than memories to guide our own education.

It is likely that observation and learning on the job will continue to serve as the foundation for preparing teaching artists. However, increased attention and reliance on teaching artists in education has led many in our field to create programs that focus on teaching artist preparation and continuing development. Like teacher education in general, professional programs in institutions of higher education and professional development of teachers already teaching are two of the primary areas in which these activities occur.

At the University of Arizona, we developed an undergraduate and graduate degree program that focuses on the theatre-teaching artist. A few other institutions around the country have similar programs that take seriously the preparation of artists for teaching. The challenges are several, and there is little research yet on the effectiveness of such programs for the field. Our clues for creating such programs come from the general efforts and research in teacher education. Much of this book relies on research in teaching and teacher education to inform the development of artistry for teaching.

The challenges have much to do with the limitations of all departments and schools of the arts in terms of resources, time, and faculty. Many departments and schools of theatre and the other arts devote their resources, time, and faculty to the preparation of artists rather than of teachers. If someone wants to teach the art form, the arts departments will provide the disciplinary background and leave the professional course work in pedagogy to colleges of education and teacher education programs. This may work fine (although many argue it does not) for those who want to teach full time in schools as arts specialists; however, the amount of time required for pedagogical course work usually limits the amount of time and experience students can gain in their content area. If one of the assumptions of the teaching artist is that he or she is a working artist as well as a teacher, it stands to reason that preparation must emphasize education as an artist as a primary goal in preparation for teaching.

One of the requirements for most faculty members in teacher education is that they have been teachers and spent at least three years teaching young people in schools or other educational settings. Teacher educators continue to work with young people while also carrying out the research expectations that most college or schools of education require. Similarly, departments and schools in the arts expect faculty members to be teaching artists although not necessarily teaching young people in education. In theatre, for example, faculty members who teach acting, design, or directing are expected to engage in professional work in their given areas. The challenge for arts education faculty who prepare teaching artists in education for young people is to continue to work as an artist, a teaching artist with young people, and to conduct research in education.

Challenges of providing strong disciplinary preparation as artists and concerns for faculty participation as teaching artists in education affect the scope of the curriculum for teaching artist preparation. In my own program, I teach two courses in performance technique: one course in improvisation and another in collaborative play development. I attempt to make visible for students my artistry for teaching by making visible the pedagogical reasons for selecting and teaching, and I ask students to design and sometimes teach their own exercises in class. In the collaborative play development course, I teach the devising process and apply it to the development of performances for young audiences. A methods course for teaching theatre as teaching artists, using examples of practice to further discussion and encourage discussion, is offered for those students wishing to enter the teaching artist profession. Students participate in field experiences as student-teaching artists in community settings and schools. Students also take courses in education, focusing on building their knowledge of schools and child development. This curriculum introduces the basics for students in the program to develop their own artistry for teaching. However, many students graduate with degrees in acting or design without courses in teaching. They may, I suspect, find themselves working as teaching artists at some time in their career. They may, like I did, learn most of what they do on the job. The responsibility for preparing those artists for teaching and for supporting those who enter the field as novice teaching artists falls to arts organizations and others to provide professional development. Fortunately, and probably due to the lack of preparation for teaching in artist preparation programs, many arts organizations and others working in the field are stepping up to meet this responsibility.

Teaching artists, like many teachers, often feel isolated and alone. Often, the teaching artist is self-employed, working in a variety of settings, putting together a pastiche of jobs to form a career, with few others to share with, grow with, and learn from. This vision of the independent artisan is part of what attracts artists to the world of teaching. However, for theatre artists, the need for community in teaching mirrors the communal nature and joy of working as an artist in theatre. The theatre-teaching artist desires belongingness, in the same way the young people we teach desire to belong to a theatre group. A first step toward professional development for teaching artists, especially those in theatre, is to build a collaborative culture of teaching artists.

As members of a shared culture, we find fellowship with others who share our realities of the working world; who speak the same language of artistry, students, learning, and teaching; and who grapple with similar problems and seek solutions. "Our realities mean what they mean because we have internalized common ways of thinking about them and talking about them" (Greene 1991, 4). At the same time, we also recognize that each one of us looks at those realities with a unique perspective and a particular location within our art form and our experiences. So within our culture, there needs to be room for diverse voices and leadership in our own development. Ongoing conversations through journals and on Internet sites provide ways for teaching artists to talk with each other on a national and global scale. In local communities, arts education organizations, such as SUAVE (*Socios Unidos para Artes Via Educación*—United Community for Arts in Education) in San Diego, offer weekly meetings with the program director to share insights and concerns and collectively share their ideas and solve problems. "Camaraderie creates a sense of program ownership and reinforces a sense of flexibility, and modeling in terms of a process of brainstorming. A culture of invention is created, valued, and reinforced" (Goldberg 2004, 22).

Building a community in which teaching artists regularly inquire into their own practice expands the notions of what it means to be a teaching artist and provides opportunities for the reflective practice so critical to the artistry of our work. In this way, teaching artists depend less on program directors or administrators telling them what to do and more on co-constructing a vision of themselves as skilled practitioners. Organizations that take time to create and support opportunities for teaching artist-led activities, such as study groups, curriculum writing, action research, and peer observations, find that the overall program and the individual teaching artist benefit.

Another key component of successful professional development is to work together to develop authentic ways of assessing and evaluating what young people are learning as a result of their practice. This practice results in overall program evaluation that stays true to the mission and goals of the program while at the same time acknowledges the individual artistry as an integral part of the whole. In this way, the program director and teaching artists become "responsive evaluators," to use Robert Stake's (1975) term, and criteria are based on "naturally-occurring responses to actual happenings" (34).

Beyond program evaluation, teaching artists also engage in research activities, either singly or in collaboration with others, which advance both their own practice and the profession as a whole. As reflective practitioner, the teaching artist is already engaged in many of the processes that characterize action research. Action research extends the reflective efforts to deliberately and consciously collect and analyze data for the purpose of understanding a particular problem or area of interest within the teaching project and to contribute to the literature on teaching and artistry. Within the action research model, the researcher identifies and formulates the focus for the project; designs methods for collecting and analyzing data; implements the research program throughout the project; and displays the data in order to share it with others. Like reflective practice in general, the research process is cyclical and is open to change and adaptation. Peter Holly distinguishes the differences between "doing research for action and doing research in/of action" (1991, 149). Research for action is conducted from a prescriptive orientation, seeking to create a database for planning. Research in action mirrors the reflection-in-action orientation, seeking to implement and analyze what is happening during the actual teaching. Research of action contributes to the evaluation of impact and effectiveness of teaching.

Displaying the data enriches the profession by contributing to the knowledge base of teaching artists, generating models of practice that describe projects accomplished in particular contexts for particular teachers and students. These models of practice become cases. Case studies are invaluable to the furthering of any profession. Students and practitioners in medicine, in law, and in teaching—to name a few—use cases, both those of others and their own, to develop their knowledge base for practice. "To call something a case is to make the claim that it is a 'case of something'" (Shulman 1986, 31). Cases not only represent the individual context and project but also must have some generalizability to the field as a whole. Cases that describe the artistry and application of artistry in the classroom provide a base from which the teaching artist develops and extends her pedagogical reasoning about teaching in future specific situations. Efforts by many teaching artists and organizations to carefully research and display their practice provide a rich resource of cases, which contribute to key conditions for transforming our practice into a profession. The cases as developed by teaching artists in practice illustrate the body of necessary knowledge and skills autonomously determined by teaching artists and provide examples of innovative practice grounded in theory. Taken as whole, examination of our practice brings us into conversation with each other and with educators in general as a way to develop and expand our field continually.

Throughout initial preparation, professional development, and teaching, the individual teaching artist relies on his or her imagination, spirit, and passion for the art form and for the students to fuel his or her commitment to arts education. However, if we want to build communities in which collaboration is promoted and individual artistry is allowed to thrive, both for members of our profession and for the young people we teach, then our work must also contribute to arts education advocacy efforts. Our research and program evaluation inform not only our own practice but arts education in general. Advocacy in education is primarily a philanthropical and political endeavor. According to *The 2002 Survey of Public Participation in the Arts,* as reviewed by Lynn Cooper in *Teaching Artist Journal,* "76% of adults participated in the arts at least one time between September 2001 and August 2002" (2004, 58). And it is safe to say that when asked, most adults will say that the arts are important to education. Parents consistently report that they want their children to participate in the arts. Schools and community organizations' ability to provide arts education for young people depends on resources that come from government funding and private donations of individuals and foundations. As teaching artists, we must use what we know about what we do and the effects of our work on young people to inform the national conversations around what is essential for our nation's schools and our young people. The National Endowment for the Arts and the Kennedy Center, so critical to the beginning of our work, continue to support and disseminate the work of teaching artists. Teaching artists must be prepared to take an active role in advocating for the arts, using their role as artists committed to teaching and as citizens committed to a democratic society.

The conceptions of artistry in practice presented in this book will, I hope, contribute to the profession by providing ways for thinking about our work as a profession, a field in which individuals develop and share their own artistry while meeting the needs of the various constituencies in which they work. Ours is a profession we choose willingly because we believe in the power of our art form and the power of the arts in education. Dewey believed, and Maxine Greene reminds us, that "what we become, what we make of ourselves, depends on what we do with our lives" (1991, 6). As we look to the future and develop our potential as teaching artists, we approach our work with care, commitment, and artistry. We engage with others to create communities of learners among both others in our profession and the young people we teach.

Appendix A

Key Exercises for Teaching

Starting and Ending Rituals

Each session begins and ends with a group ritual. To begin, students change into the working clothes and enter the space ready to work. At the end of the session, students gather in a circle and acknowledge the collective work before changing into street clothes.

Procedure (5 minutes at beginning and end)

1. Signal the time to begin with a bell or clap.

2. Students remove their outer garments or leave the room and dress in the chosen work clothes.

3. Students enter the space, acknowledge the presence of others, and find a spot to work that allows them room for exploration without infringing on the space of others.

4. At the end of the session, students gather in a circle. In unison, they raise their arms over their heads, taking in the breath as they do. Holding the breath, we try to make eye contact with as many people as we can in the circle, saying "thank you" with our eyes to acknowledge the individual contributions of all. Releasing the breath, we bring our arms to our sides and end with a quick bow. Students then leave the space to change back into street clothes.

Chase

One student sends a sound and a movement around the circle. The goal is to create a wave-like movement and sound without interruption or pauses in between. The exercise introduces the collective and physical nature of the work we do in theatre.

Procedure (10–25 minutes, depending on size of group)

1. Once students have formed the circle, the leader begins by sending a sound and a movement. The student to the right or left repeats the sound and movement, sending it around the circle.

2. The one who initiated the sound and movement repeats it, and the next one changes the sound and movement and sends it in the same direction around the circle.

3. After the exercise, immediately ask students to comment on what they noticed, what challenges we had as individuals and as a group.

Variation: Use a hand clap instead of sound and movement. Once everyone is comfortable with the hand clap variation, encourage students to disrupt the direction and the hand clap pattern. Everyone in the circle responds to the changes, either by sending it along the circle or by changing it themselves.

Back to Back

This exercise encourages students to work with many members in the group. It is also a quick and engaging way to divide into smaller groups. Students move about the space, finding different partners and interacting with each partner in a variety of ways.

Procedure (5–10 minutes)

1. Students move about the space, making eye contact but without physical contact or sound. The leader calls out "back to back." Students find a partner and stand back to back with that person. At another signal, the partners dissolve and the group moves about the space again.

2. Each time the group breaks into partners, the leader can call out different body positions: foot to foot, shoulder to shoulder, head to head, and so forth. It is not necessary to stay back to back each time.

3. Increase the difficulty by varying the body positions: shoulder to knee, hand to foot, hip to elbow, head to foot, and the like. Encourage students to accomplish the physical positions without talking to each other and as quickly and efficiently as possible.

4. Once students are familiar with the exercise, the leader can signal the group to form partners nonverbally—using a hand clap, a drumbeat,

or a bell. Students find a partner and assume a physical relationship without talking or knowing ahead of time what position they will form together. Another signal releases the partners and the group resumes moving about the space.

Variation: Increase the size of the groups. Rather than working as partners, encourage students to form groups of four or five and find physical relationships between all members of the group, still without talking or knowing ahead of time what position they will form together.

Stop and Go

The goal of this exercise is observing and listening with the body. It is a wonderful way to see who has trouble working within the group and who does not. It also provides a reminder of the collective nature of the work whenever working together becomes difficult.

Procedure (5–15 minutes)
1. Students move about the space without talking or touching. To begin, the leader calls out, "stop," and everyone stops in position. The leader then calls out, "go," and everyone begins moving again.

2. Once students are familiar, the leader does not call out. Rather, when one person in the group stops, everyone stops. Once everyone is still, any person in the group can start moving and the whole group responds.

3. As the exercise progresses, encourage the group to try moving at different speeds. After the exercise, discuss how well the group worked together.

Playground Ball Toss in a Circle

This exercise utilizes two playground balls to physicalize the collaborative relationship between actors working on a play. It is a deceptively difficult exercise and not one for playing with children who have not yet developed hand–eye coordination.

Procedure (10–20 minutes)
Materials: two large rubber balls

1. Students work in a circle. The leader (and later the students) stands in the center of the circle and gently tosses one ball out to someone in the circle. That person tosses the ball back to the leader in the center. The ball moves around the circle, returning to the center each time. Begin by moving around the circle, and then vary the pattern by throwing the ball randomly to any given person in the circle. Throw the ball underhanded. Encourage everyone to work to create a rhythm for the ball by catching the ball with both hands, making a slapping sound.

2. Once the group is comfortable throwing and catching the one ball, work on changing the leader in the center, without interrupting the movement of the ball around the circle. One person from the circle moving into the center, signaling to the person in the center that a change is taking place, accomplishes the transition of leader. There is no verbal communication throughout the exercise.

3. After doing this for a bit, stop and ask students to think of themselves as actors in a play. One actor has a line or a moment on stage while everyone else is supporting that actor; open to receive at any moment what the actor in the center gives, and responding by giving back. Repeat the exercise again keeping this metaphor in mind.

4. After mastering the transitions between circle and leaders, introduce a second ball. The person in the center throws the first ball to the circle at the same time one person in the circle throws the second ball to the center. The goal is for the balls to leave and arrive simultaneously so that one sound (the slap against the ball) and one rhythm are created by the whole group. Continue to work around the circle and on the transitions from one leader to another with the two balls.

The Truth About Me: Exploring Who We Are

Once skills are identified, this exercise is a fun way to share them.

Procedure (10–20 minutes, depending on size of group)
1. Students sit in a circle on chairs, minus one. One student begins in the center of the circle. The group uses the sentence stem: "The truth about me is that I can (*naming something on their list*)." If any student shares the same skill, he must get up and either move to another chair or, if none is available, find himself in the center. The exercise

continues until everyone has had at least one turn in the center. While the exercise is going, the leader writes down all of the skills mentioned on large sheets of paper.

2. After the exercise, the group reviews the collected list of skills and adds names to the inventory to construct a master list.

Extensions: Working from the master list, students choose a skill and working either individually or with others from the list, they compose a short demonstration of the skill. Students sit in a circle to share their demonstrations with the rest of the group.

Snap and Click

This is an excellent exercise to introduce students to tableaux work.

Procedure (10 minutes)

1 Everyone stands around the space in a neutral position. The leader calls out an emotion or occupation or activity (i.e., happy, doctor, painting a wall). When the leader calls out "snap," students assume a pose that reflects the word and freeze. Students hold the pose until leader calls out, "click," (as in taking a photograph).

2. Students return to neutral and the leader calls out another word.

Two-Person Tableaux Work

Encourage students to work quickly without talking or discussion, building on each other to investigate possibilities. The point is to move through the activity quickly. Don't complete the image or attempt to construct a scene or ministry. Encourage students to pay attention to proximity, focus, and levels.

Procedure (10–20 minutes)

1. Students work with a partner. The two students meet, shake hands, and freeze. One person moves out of the frozen picture (the other stays frozen) and creates a new physical relationship with the other to create a new frozen picture.

2. The other then releases from the picture and, using the new posture of the other, creates a new physical relationship.

3. The exercise continues in this way with each partner finding new physical relationships with the other.

4. Change partners several times so everyone in the group has the opportunity to work with several different people.

5. After working simultaneously, ask partners to share their work with the whole group. Ask students to notice and label relationships they see.

Relationships in Action

Repetitions push us to break an action down and find an artistic expression of the human intention behind it. This gives the actors the opportunity to examine choices in stage picture and composition within the "text" or story being told.

Procedure (10–20 minutes)
1. Think of an activity; enter the circle and begin doing the activity (painting a fence, mopping a floor, drawing a picture).

2. Another person enters and adds to the same activity, concentrating on connecting in relation to what the first person is doing.

3. Continue adding until it seems complete and then freeze the action.

4. Ask the group to create a title for the "scene."

Four Corners

Students work quickly to connect with each other around a story or an idea. Keep the pace moving. Repeat several times around one idea.

Procedure (20–25 minutes)
1. Brainstorm a list of words, characters, or scenes based on a story or idea.

2. Divide students into four groups, and ask one group to stand in one of the four corners of the space.

3. Leader calls out something from the list. One person from each corner—one at a time—runs into the center and forms a shape until a tableau is formed with four bodies—freeze.

4. Dynamize the tableau by tapping one student at a time in the tableau. When they are tapped, ask them to speak a phrase that best fits their pose.

5. When the leader repeats the word—the tableau dissolves.

Shadows

This exercise builds on the familiar mirror exercise and encourages students to begin moving about the space; still "listening" to the partner they are working with.

Procedure (10–20 minutes)
1. Ask students to find a partner. Using the metaphor of shadows, ask students to begin walking with one partner, shadowing the other as they walk. At a signal from the teacher, the person leading turns and immediately becomes the shadow of the other. Encourage students to continue the movement and not to stop in the transition.

2. Once students are comfortable with shadow walking, encourage pairs to initiate different movements—using levels, varying rhythms, leading with different parts of the body, conducting small activities (tying a shoe, washing the floor). Continue shadowing and changing shadowing throughout the exercise.

3. After the work, use observations to discuss the differences between mirrors and shadows.

Triangles

This exercise is beautiful to watch and often becomes a technique I use in staging of a performance, especially when working with larger groups.

Procedure (20–25 minutes)
1. Divide the class into groups of three. (If you have more, groups can also work in fours, in the shape of a diamond, rather than a triangle.) Ask them to position themselves in the shape of a triangle. Each person forms a point of the triangle. Ask two students to face one point of the triangle. The person at that point initiates a movement and the other two shadow those movements.

2. Either on her own or at a signal from the teacher, the person rotates to the left or right, which changes the point of the triangle. The new point (or person) continues with the movement, transforming it slowly into her own series of movements, until she rotates, changing the point again.

3. Allow the triangles to continue for several revolutions, encouraging students to experiment with levels, speeds, and quality of the movement.

4. Share the work with each other, asking students to observe each group's ability to pass movement from one point to the next without interruption and to describe the qualities created by the whole group as they move together. Ask students to consider possible relationships between the three.

Using Artifacts with Tableaux

This exercise uses physical work to explore collected artifacts for generating ideas/material for performance.

Procedure (20–30 minutes)

1. Using examples from photographs, poems, or narrative text, divide the class into groups of four or five. Hand out artifacts and ask the groups to create a tableau based on the artifact. Have students build the tableau by having one take a pose, another student add to the pose, creating a physical relationship with the first. Continue until the group has formed a tableau.

2. Once all of the groups have formed tableau, share them by having one group present their tableau while the other groups walk around the tableau, writing a title and a two- to three-line story of the tableau on note cards. They place the cards on the floor around the tableau. When finished, the students in tableau relax and gather the cards.

3. Repeat the exercise with all of the groups.

4. Working in their respective groups, the students read over the cards and select one. Each group returns to the tableau and improvises a short scene—based on the title and "story" on the cards. Encourage students to progress through the story, keeping words or dialogue to a minimum.

5. Share the scenes with each other, observing how the groups used their tableau and the suggestions from the others to tell the story and how relationships changed or remained the same.

Improvisation with Portraits

I've often found that using portraits helps struggling students unlock physical ideas for creating character, even if the portrait is not directly related to the content or never is used outside of the improvisational stage. Putting diverse historical "portraits" (a knight, a queen, a farm woman in a kitchen in the 1930s) together in contemporary locations provokes some interesting scenes and encourages students to reach beyond their own physical and vocal range to play with character and relationship.

Procedure (30–40 minutes)
1. Students choose a particular portrait and base their character choices on what they see in the portrait.

2. Each student creates a physicalization of the portrait and writes a two- to three-sentence monologue.

3. Students share monologues with each other.

4. Group three to four characters together in a specific location and ask them to improvise a scene.

Characters in Relationship with Setting and Others

This exercise asks students to put together the elements of CROW (character, relationship, objective, where) into one scene. It is usually a good idea to work on one element at a time in the beginning, adding as students become more comfortable with the exercise.

Procedure (10–20 minutes)
1. Ask students to mill about the space, walking and making eye contact but not physically or vocally interacting with others.

2. As students mill about, ask them to select one of the skills from their personal inventory. At a signal from the teacher, prompt students to

begin doing the activity, exploring the physical character that emerges as they do the skills.

3. After time for individual exploration, ask everyone to move to one side. Set up a room and endow it with a location (i.e., a waiting room in a doctor's office, a post office). Use chairs, tables, boxes, and so on to help define the location. Ask students to enter the space one at a time, as the character they just created. The goal is to interact with the setting in a realistic way while still maintaining the character. Write down the characters as the students proceed.

4. Using your list and the observations of students, arrange characters in partners. As a group, brainstorm a list of relationships for the characters (parent–child, doctor–patient, employer–employee, etc.). Ask partners to choose a relationship and improvise a scene that might occur, still using the skills of the character. Allow everyone to play at once for a time to generate ideas. Side coach students to make specific and strong choices.

5. Share the scenes with each other. Discuss the conflicts between characters and situations that arise and if any resolutions were achieved. At the beginning, resolutions, if present, are usually weak and easily won. After discussion, ask students to return to their scenes and improvise toward resolution, making sure resolutions are earned through dialogue and emotional involvement of the characters.

6. Share the scenes again, this time focusing on how resolutions were achieved. Record key dialogue and scenes for future use.

Appendix B

Tools for Assessment and Evaluation

Processfolio

Items to Include

- Written journal entries—either prompted by questions from the group or directed by the teaching artist based on the task at hand.
- Records of the improvisations for generating material for the devised performance—these could be written notes or video recordings.
- Research collected on the topic at hand.
- Formal evaluations of performance—done to evaluate how well students are incorporating critical skills into their daily work based on criteria that arise from the task at hand and are accomplished by the teacher, by peers, and through self-evaluation.
- Notes of the critical response process—questions and suggestions for future development of the work.
- Designs of space for performance based on ideas generated from discussions and material generated.
- Working scripts of final performance with individual notations of character development and blocking.
- Reflections on final performance with anecdotes from comments of fellow performers, the audience, and the director.

Criteria for Evaluation

- The regularity and completeness of the individual entries
- The awareness of their own strengths and weaknesses
- Their capacity to reflect accurately the goals for the work at hand

- Their ability to consider self and other critiques to improve their own practice
- Their resourcefulness in solving problems and finding outside resources
- Their ability to relate theatre exploration to other content areas
- Their sensitivity to their own process and the process of others
- Their discipline in terms of approaching the work seriously

Performance Assessments

Checklists and Rating Scales

Arts Connection in New York City developed a checklist for observing students in improvisations for the purposes of identifying talent in theatre arts (see Oreck, Baum, and Owen, 2004). The checklist was narrowed to four categories.

Physical Awareness
Responds with whole body
Is in control of body parts
Uses and perceives vocal qualities
Can use voice flexibility
Wants to be heard and understood
Is aware of space
Notices details
Observes carefully
Seems relaxed
Is unembarrassed

Focus/Commitment
Gives energy
Takes risks
Participates fully
Perseveres
Focuses eyes on the imagined environment and other players
Recalls instructions
Can revise and improve own work

Imagination
Offers ideas
Comes up with original or unusual suggestions

Finds multiple solutions
Makes the situation real
Solves problems
Sees the whole picture
Invents dramatic situations
Has a sense of effective timing

Collaboration

Works with others
Responds to the audience
Accepts the rules of the exercises
Listens to teachers and peers
Gives helpful suggestions
Takes a leadership role

Notice that the descriptors are behaviors that can be observed in performance. As a checklist, the teacher observes the individual within a performance exercise and marks whether the behavior is noticed or not noticed. The checklist can be used as a rating scale. The numerical score is based on the total number of behaviors observed in each category (i.e., 3 out of 4). Looking across the four categories, the teacher can also give a holistic rating such as 1 to 5 (with 5 being the best) for each student to capture intuitive impressions for the overall performance.

Rubrics

Teaching artists and administrators at Arizona Theatre Company developed a rubric to evaluate individual student performance interpreting a written monologue as a way to measure student progress in their summer production program for high school students. This rubric is based on a scale of 1 to 4, with 4 being the highest score. On the first day of the program, students were given an unfamiliar thirty-second monologue. They were provided one minute to peruse the rubric skill list and two minutes to prepare the text for an individual audition with the evaluator. On the final day of the program, students were asked to repeat the exercise, using unfamiliar monologues and the same rubric skills. Pre- and postscores for each individual showed student progress in the identified skill areas. Taken together, the students scores were used as part of the overall program evaluation.

Skill	Score			
	4	**3**	**2**	**1**
Actors demonstrate poise and present themselves with appropriate audition protocol.	Self-confidence and an appropriate demonstration of energy are always evident.	Self-confidence and an appropriate demonstration of energy are sometimes evident.	Self-confidence or an appropriate demonstration of energy is seldom demonstrated.	Neither self-confidence nor an appropriate demonstration of energy is demonstrated.
Actors understand the technical use of body and voice to establish minimum audition performance standards.	The actor is always audible and physically open to the listener.	The actor is sometimes audible and physically open to the listener.	The actor is seldom audible or physically open to the listener.	The actor is never audible or physically open to the listener.
Actors employ physical choices and changes to create character.	The actor always demonstrates physical choices and changes to create a character body.	The actor sometimes demonstrates physical choices and changes to create a character body.	The actor seldom demonstrates physical choices or changes to create a character body.	The actor never demonstrates physical choices or changes to create a character body.
Actors employ vocal choices and changes to create character.	The actor always demonstrates choices or changes in pitch and rate to create a character voice.	The actor sometimes demonstrates choices or changes in pitch and rate to create a character voice.	The actor seldom demonstrates choices or changes in pitch or rate to create a character voice.	The actor never demonstrates choices or changes in pitch or rate to create a character voice.
Actors utilize vocal and physical characterization to pursue character objectives.	The actor always demonstrates evidence of character wants through physicalization and vocalization.	The actor sometimes demonstrates evidence of character wants through physicalization and vocalization.	The actor seldom demonstrates evidence of character wants through physicalization or vocalization.	The actor never demonstrates evidence of character wants through physicalization or vocalization.

Courtesy of Arizona Theatre Company, 2005

# ppendix C

In the Year of the Immigrant

Selections written by Gretchen Orsland and Barbara McKean
Music and lyrics written by Joseph Seserko
Performed by students in the Seattle School District, Seattle, Washington

SONG: "This Country's Getting Crowded"

This country's getting crowded
Do we have enough space?
We've got a lot of different people living in this place.
This country's getting louder
There are many new sounds
We've got a lot of different music traveling around.
Different music, changing chords.
Different tempo, changing words
Different music, changing sounds
Different rhythm, all around.

Questions to Newcomers

Do you have any money?
Why are you coming here?
Do you have a passport?
How people are in your family?
Do you have a sickness?
Have you had your shots?
How long do you intend to stay?
Are you a spy?

Packing Scenes with Away From/Coming To

Away from the place where flowers bloom.
Coming to big buildings.
Away from my home.
Going to sunshine and good friends.
Away from soldiers in uniforms with tanks and guns.
Coming to people with accents.
Away from where the rivers flow.
Coming to weather that can't make up its mind.
Away from my Grandfather's grave.
Coming to streets paved with gold.
Away from the things I shall never forget.

In the Year of the Boar and Jackie Robinson:

Grandmother scene (Lord 1984, 13–14)
Grandfather scene (Lord 1984, 17–19)

SONG: "Moving"

Moving moving moving moving
Moving moving moving moving
People that come from distant lands
Hoping that people understand
Different customs, different language
Moving moving moving moving
Moving moving moving moving
Moving away from distant places
Moving away from other faces
Moving in hope of finding a better way
A way with different traditions
A way with freedom of religions
To settle in a new world and to have a better home
A way for better education
A way for better occupations
A way to find a better nation

To call home
Moving moving moving moving
Moving moving moving moving
Immigrants bring us new perspectives
Moving our world in different directions
Bringing together different ways of life
Bringing bringing bringing bringing
Bringing bringing bringing bringing
Welcome the changing forms of culture
Welcome the changing forms of fashion
Moving in hope of finding a better way
A way with different traditions
A way with freedom of religions
To settle in a new world and to have a better home
A way for better education
A way for better occupations
A way to settle in a new world
And to have a better home
For better education
For better occupations
Together in a nation
Together in a nation we call home.

Transportation Tableaux

Ellis Island

My first impressions of the New World will always remain in my memory. Particularly that hazy October morning when I first saw Ellis Island. Our steamer, FLORIDA, fourteen days out of Naples, filled to capacity with 1600 natives of Italy, had weathered one of the worst storms in our captain's memory; and glad we were, both children and grown ups to leave the open sea and come at last through the Narrows into the bay. My mother, my stepfather, my brother and my two sisters, all of us together, happy that we had come through the storm safely, holding hands, arms around each other, looked with wonder on this miraculous land of our dreams. My brother and I held tightly to Stepfather's hands, while my sisters clung to Mother. Passengers all about us were crowding against the rail. The air was filled with conversations, sharp cries, laughs and cheers. Mothers and Fathers lifted babies so that they too could see, off to the left, the Statue of Liberty. (Corsi 1935, 3)

Train Scene
In the Year of the Boar and Jackie Robinson (Lord 1984, 24).

Letters from America
ALL: Dear friend,

#1: I can hardly wait for you to arrive. There are lots of things to do here in America. We play games like baseball (our national pastime). That's where you hit a ball with a big stick and run like crazy...

#2: And games like football, where you catch a ball and run like crazy...

#3: And a game called basketball, where you try to throw a ball into a basket.

#1: A big thing in America is the mall. This is a place with lots of stores and where people and kids hang out. You'll love the mall.

#2: But there are some bad things here too. Like drugs. We have choices. We all have a chance to say yes, no, or maybe. And there are times when our government makes mistakes. But we are allowed to speak up and criticize.

#3: I think you will like it here once you get used to it. It feels good to live here.

ALL: We are looking forward to seeing you. Have a safe trip. Your friend.

SONG: " Things American"

Restaurants, schools, gyms, computers, movies, Nintendo's,
Forty-one Presidents.
Cartoons, hats, sunglasses, backpacks, pencils, bikes,
Coffee cake.
Root beer, math, science, reading, health, umbrellas,
Calendars and guns.
Chairs, pillows, lamps, soup and nuts.

Welcoming Gifts

Welcome. Come in. Make yourself comfortable.
I give you food—good food.

I give you warm clothes for the winter.
I give you shelter from the rain.
I give you my friendship. Even on the weekends.
I give you candy in noisy wrappers.
I give you my TV guide (with all my favorite programs
    underlined).
I give you the combination: 14-5-87.
I give you my smiles.
I give you my laughter.
I give you diamonds in the sky.
I give you a fourteen-karat-gold kind of dream.

SONG: "Carl"

Chorus:
Carl is a new kid in our class
And he is not the same as us
He looks a little strange to us
We cannot say his last name
Carl came here from far away
Exactly where we cannot say
Cause even when he tells us where
We cannot pronounce the name.
Verse:
He wears different shoes
And different shirts
And different kinds of glasses
So whenever Carl sits at lunch
Everybody passes
Repeat Chorus
Verse:
He's got different ways of saying things
With different kinds of words
It's an interesting language but
I have never heard it.
He likes different songs, with different sounds
A different kind of music

I was listening the other day
I think I really liked it.
Carl is a new kid in our class
And he is not the same as us
But he can teach a lot to us
Everyone is not the same.
Carl came here from far away
Exactly where we cannot say
But he may show us where someday
And we'll learn to say his name.

SPOKEN SONG: "Food March"

Pizza, hot dogs, apple pie
Big Macs, French-fries
Finger lickin' southern fried
That's the food America buys
Lasagna, spaghetti and parmesan cheese
Pesto, linguine and macaroni.
Burrito, tacos
Fajitas, nachos
Lox, bagels, kosher, kosher,
Lox, bagels, kosher, kosher
Sau-er-kraut, sau-er-kraut
Sau-er-kraut, sau-er-kraut
Pizza, hot dogs, apple pie
Big Macs, French-fries
Finger lickin' southern fried
American food is every kind.

In the Year of the Boar and Jackie Robinson

Baseball scene (Lord 1984, 76–82)
Mrs. Rappaport scene (Lord 1984, 92)

I'm Proud to Be An American monologues

Reprise of "This Country's Getting Crowded"

 # ppendix D

Boundless: A Musical Across Borders

> Between east and west, past and future,
> We lay these boundless hopes for peace.

Book by Carl Sander; Music and lyrics by Carl Sander, Suzanne Grant, and Volodia Vladimirov. Produced by the Seattle Peace Theatre in collaboration with the Young Actors Musical Theater of Moscow, Russia, and the Children and Youth Theatre of Zurich, Switzerland, and performed July 16–19, 1992 in Seattle, Washington.

The play takes place in a nameless space. Along the back of the stage is scaffolding, creating levels for the action of the play. Hidden underneath the scaffolding are pieces of wood, fabric, and other found objects used in the construction of the ship. At the beginning the stage is empty except for a suitcase containing a rolled-up drawing, a shirt, a hat, a water bottle, a toothbrush, a passport, a pinecone, and a diary.

Each group is costumed in like colors: The ill group is dressed in shades of yellow, the war group in shades of red, and the intolerance group in shades of gray. Members of the groups carry backpacks or makeshift bundles. The play is spoken in English although at times characters repeat phrases in German or Russian. Choruses in songs are repeated in German or Russian.

Cast of Characters (character names are based on the actors' first names)

RACHEL—a traveler seeking information about the past

NANETTE—the scribe who wrote about the troubles in a diary

KARIN—best friend of Nanette, who died during the troubles and reappears as a ghost

PHILIP—a would-be leader of the groups seeking escape

SABINA—Philip's partner

SEBASTIAN—a lone traveler who disdains the company of others

GROUP OF ILL—refugees from disease (*Andrea, Caroline, Anna, Michael, Julia, Ani, Yurislav, Tania, Bryna, Polina, Yuri, and Marguerita*)

GROUP OF WAR—refugees from war (*Alona, Genia, Noelle, Josh, Azizi, Bryan, Ilona, Svetlana, Nadia, Tigran, Sabrina, Mona, Miriam, and Jenny*)

GROUP OF INTOLERANCE—those who seek sameness in the face of difference (*Jonathan, Denise, Emily, Marc, David, Autumn, Rowen, Lukas, Sara, Mira, Roman, and Lera*)

CHORUS—10 young actors from the three theatre groups

Prologue: Escape from Tomorrow

In dim lights, the whole cast surrounds the stage, all in the shadows, to form a large semi-circle. They clap once. The house lights go out. They clap again. Rachel, Lera, Josh, Emily, and Julia run downstage as if playing a game. They discover the items on the stage.

RACHEL: Look. What is this?

LERA: A hat.

JOSH: *(picking up the shirt and water bottle)* Someone must have left these here.

EMILY: *(picks up the toothbrush in disgust)* It seems as if they've been here a while.

RACHEL: Here is a book. It's a diary.

LERA: Let's read it.

JOSH: No! That's not polite.

EMILY: Whoever left it is long gone.

JULIA: Read it.

RACHEL: *(opens the book and reads)* It is a time of great trouble and promise for peace, but no one can find peace.

LERA: Oh, that's an old story. *(Picks up the pinecone and tosses it to the side of the stage)* Let's go.

EMILY: Yes. It's no concern of ours. *(Sees the passport and puts it in her pocket).*

RACHEL: You all run along if you like. I'm going to figure this out.

The others exit. Rachel sits and reads silently. As she does, the cast sings.

Escape from Tomorrow

> *Every time I turn around*
> *I care a little less*
> *With every war and every heartbreak*
> *I face another test*
> *I fear the future's beating drum*
> *Has a message just for me*
> *Warning of the monster I may become*
> *Shaped by history*
> *We gotta get away*
> *Escape from tomorrow*
> *It gets closer by the day*
> *Gotta get away/gotta get away*
> *The situation's looking bad*
> *The heat is on*
> *Trees are tumbling down*
> *For greed*
> *Have we come so far*
> *For what we do not need*
> *Today I saw*
> *A child laugh at someone's death*
> *Today I heard a wicked joke*
> *Today I lost a good friend's trust*
> *Today my young heart was broke*

Cast claps again and exits. Left behind on stage are Nanette (who picks up the suitcase as if she is ready to travel) and Rachel.

Scene One: Searching for a Better Place

RACHEL: *(reading)* I also was wounded. My friend, Karin, whom I had trusted with so many little confidences was dead. A victim of the troubles. And so I too entered the flood, left behind the only home I had known, and sought a better life. *(She continues reading silently)*

Philip and Sabina enter and stop by Nanette, surveying the scene.

NANETTE: This place is hateful to me. It once brought us so much joy.

Philip and Sabina are unmoved by her display of emotion. The ghost of Karin enters and stands beside Philip and Sabina.

NANETTE: *(looking toward the heavens)* Good-bye, my good friend.

The ghost of Karin moves to sit by Nanette, who does not see her but senses her presence.

RACHEL: *(reading)* I remember the day we went to a neighboring city to buy Karin new boots. How happy she was.

The group of the ill enter and travel past her like a group of plague victims, coughing and wearing ragged clothes.

CAROLINE: *(to Nanette)* I cannot find my mother.

NANETTE: Run if you can. You will not find any answers here. You are fools! If you had seen with these eyes, or felt with this heart, you would crumble into dust.

Sebastian enters and stands alone.

SEBASTIAN: Well, what have we here? The French soccer team? *(The Ill group reaches out for help)* What is the matter with you?

ANI: We are sick

NOELLE: I cannot see.

YURISLAV: My leg

TANIA: Help us.

SEBASTIAN: Shut up. Shut up all of you. You should be ashamed. You are dragging yourselves down. The world is yours to pluck. Get out and get ahead. Pick yourselves up and work for a better life. *(The group does not respond)* You are criminals all of you! Lazy good for nothings. You sicken me.

Sebastian exits. Philip and Sabina approve of his attitude.

The group of the Ill rises to exit. Nanette looks after them as if deciding whether or not to follow.

KARIN: *(speaking to Rachel)* They are fleeing the disease and hunger in their land. They are afraid no one will care for them when they are ill. *(softly to Nanette)* Perhaps this is where you must start.

Nanette does not seem to hear her but responds anyway, picks up her bags, and follows.

RACHEL: Please. Am I supposed to follow you?

KARIN: You may go where you wish.

Rachel is about to go with them, when Philip stops her.

PHILIP: (*not so much angry as evil*) Hey, you. You should come with us. We know the way.
SABINA: Yes. We know the way.

They back Rachel downstage.

PHILIP: I know the way. (*points to Sabina*) Her, I'm not so sure about.
SABINA: You would be lost without me.

Philip raises his hand as if to strike Sabina, but she slaps him first. At the sound, Rachel runs off.

PHILIP: Look! Now we've lost her. You silly girl.
SABINA: Don't trifle with me.
PHILIP: What are we to do now?
SABINA: (*looking offstage*) Never mind about them. Here are new fish to catch.

The group of War enters quickly from both sides of the stage. They stop and regard one another.

ILONA: Do you have milk for my baby?
SVETLANA: Yes. What a beautiful child.
ILONA: Thank you.

Svetlana steps forward toward Ilona with a bottle of milk. Azizi holds Svetlana back.

AZIZI: (*speaking to Ilona*) Your father threw us in jail.
ILONA: Your father killed my boyfriend.
NADIA: (*speaking to Ilona*) Your father stole our land.

Azizi releases Svetlana. Silence. Svetlana gives the baby the bottle. She drinks. No fight.

GENIA: We are trying to escape the troubles.
TIGRAN: We heard it is better in the mountains.
GENIA: May we join you?
PHILIP: (*breaking in to the conversation*) Of course. We must all travel together.
SABINA: Yes. Follow us.
PHILIP: And we must hurry. Hurry!

They exit, following Philip and Sabina.

Rachel enters carrying the book. She looks about. She is lost.

The group of intolerance crosses the stage once silently and very fast, a large group on the move.

RACHEL: Excuse me. Where are you going? Can I join you? Excuse me.

They ignore her and depart. She sits and opens the book and reads silently. The intolerance group enters again, singing:

The Other
> They said we were
> The other they said
> They were the chosen
> Your color is bad
> Your sex is sick
> Your beliefs are wicked
> Your hopes are impossible
> Your dreams are silly
> Your life is wrong
> No room for you
> No food for you
> No place for your ideas
> You are the other
> We will not put up
> With you any more
> Shut up
> Get out
> Be silent
> Or die.

At the end, Rachel slams the book shut, and they run off, silently. Rachel is about to run off after them, when Sebastian enters. He is ill and coughing; his clothes are ragged. Rachel approaches him with an offer of comfort and is rebuffed. Rachel looks around the empty space and exits. Sebastian coughs and exits.

Scene Two: Building the Ship

Philip/Sabina, Karin, Nanette enter and keep their distance from the others, watching.

The three groups (ill, war, intolerance) enter from different sides of the stage. As they meet each other, they speak.

GENIA: Where are you going?

ANI: This way. To the city

GENIA: We just came from there. There is fighting in the streets.

NOELLE: Where are you going?

GENIA: There. To the mountains.

DENISE: There are people who will hate you as soon as shake
  your hand.

EMILY: We just came from there.

ANI: Where are you going?

NOELLE: There, to the ocean.

ROWEN: No one will help you there.

Everyone starts speaking at once. Music begins. The groups sing.

You Can't Go There Anymore

We've turned our troubles into bones
Ground our blades on the howling stone
Cut our ties brother to brother
Turned our sisters on each other
Turned our backs on our common blood
Opened the gates let loose the flood
Chorus: Listen to me
> *It's not the same*
> *Terror reigns*
> *Believe me*
> *It's not like it was before*
> *You can't go there*
> *You can't go there*
> *You can't go there anymore*
The tide has turned the beach is dry
Cries of engines fill the sky
Duck your head as death walks by
Cover your heart. Hide the pain
Take a breath. Go insane
Repeat Chorus.

*Everyone falls down in exhaustion. Philip and Sabina exit smiling. Nanette
and Karin rest. Rachel enters with the book.*

RACHEL: (*reading*) Large groups formed and camped. Plans for a better
life were dreamed. (*The groups find places to sleep*) But often they were
lost in the confusion of sleep.

Sounds of gunfire. One person from the war groups wakes and wakes up others in the group to begin work on building the ship. They finish and return to sleep.

Sounds of ambulance sirens. One person from the ill group wakes and wakes up others in the group to begin work on building the ship, changing what the first group had done. They finish and return to sleep.

Sounds of an angry mob. One person from the intolerance group wakes and wakes up others in the group to begin work on building the ship, changing what the second group had done. They finish and return to sleep.

During the ship building, the chorus enters upstage and sings.

If Only
> The bombs are getting closer
> They're looking just for me
> My end is getting closer,
> I'm not who I used to be
> The sky is getting closer
> My nightmare's getting closer
> It's darker than the sea

By the end of the song, everyone has returned to sleep. Morning comes, the sun rises and the groups get up. Each one goes to where they think their ship is and discover the changes others have made to the ship.

> MICHAEL: You kids! Can't you leave anything alone?
> JOSH: Oh, good. Really good. You broke it.
> MARC: What do you mean? We broke it?
> DIANA: It didn't look like this when we were through.
> ROMAN: My beautiful work. Lost, destroyed. Now I will never
> grow up to be a man!
> EMILY: Oh, get over yourself!

Philip and Sabina entering, laughing. They sing.

It's Not So Easy
> TOGETHER: *It's not so easy to get away*
> *To find a land of peace*
> *You must pay*
> *Reason and plan*

> *Work and pray*
> *It's not so easy to get away*

PHILIP: *Your silly dreams will get you nowhere*
> *Any place you want to go I've been there*
> *The walls are high and the price is dear*
> *And danger is always very near.*

SABINA: *The road is littered with the likes of you*
> *But those that get by are all too few*
> *You must have a plan, a plan that's new*
> *And in my mind I have a plan or two.*

TOGETHER: *It's not so easy to get away*
> *To find a land of peace*
> *You must pay*
> *Reason and plan*
> *Work and pray*
> *It's not so easy to get away*

SABINA: *Do you believe in a promised land?*
> *I can get you there, take my hand*
> *Pass my palm with a dollar or two*
> *My promise is I'll get you through.*

PHILIP: *I have maps to foreign places*
> *I know the dignitaries' faces*
> *Follow me and you need never fear*
> *On your own you'll never get here.*

TOGETHER: *It's not so easy to get away*
> *To find a land of peace*
> *You must pay*
> *Reason and plan*
> *Work and pray*
> *It's not so easy, it's not so easy, it's not so easy*
> *To get away*

Nanette opens her suitcase, takes out a large drawing, and unfurls it. Rachel walks over and takes the plan, laying it out on the floor.

> Philip: *(takes the plan from Rachel)* Yes, you see. Now here is a plan. *(He reads the plan and directs the groups to begin working)* One. Two. Three.

Sabina congratulates Rachel, and shows her where to read in the diary.

> Rachel: *(reading)* And so we set to work on our escape vessel. Our ship that would take us far from our fears.

Everyone starts building the ship. Philip and Sabina supervise the work.

> DAVID: Hey! Someone took my shirt.
> AUTUMN: Stop! Stop! Somebody took David's shirt!
> AZIZI: So?
> AUTUMN : We must discover the criminal.
> ROMAN: But how would we know who it is?
> DAVID: Who took my shirt?
> BRYAN: We don't have time. The world is collapsing around us.
> AZIZI: He's right. We don't have time.
> ROWEN: A quick trial and a speedy execution.
> YURISLAV: We've got to keep working.
> TANIA: Yes, we must work.

Everyone falls into arguing. The cry of a baby is heard. Silence. Everyone turns to look at Ilona with the baby. Ilona, Svetlana, Nadia, Julia, and others sing.

Little One Mine

> Little one mine
> Close your eyes
> All your troubles
> Loose in dreaming
> You hold the keys
> To memories
> All adventures
> Lie before you
> Blankets warm for you
> Here's my wish for you
> That we never shall part
> Little one mine
> Smile so divine
> Lose your troubles
> In dreaming

> AZIZI: *(takes his shirt off and hands it to David)* Here. You're
>   welcome to anything I have.
> PHILIP: You must work. Work!

They all return to working on the ship.

> DAVID: Hey! Someone took my orange!

Everyone reaches into their bag, grabs an orange, and throws it at David.

Nanette crosses to David and picks up the oranges. She gives one to David and bags the others. Walks back to Karin.

RACHEL: *(reading)* We learned to share our resources and although I struggled with the others, I still remained alone. However, I felt as if in my deepest loneliness, someone was drawing me forward.

CAROLINE: *(looking out into space)* Out there. Yes. In the heart of the void, the night, dark, I search. Always I am looking for my mother.

All stop working and look out into space.

LUKAS: Shut up! Shut up and get back to work!

They start working.

LUKAS: *(struggles with rope, stops, and looks out)* My father would know how to tie this knot. Where is my father?

All stop working and look out into space.

CAROLINE: My mother was with me in the grocery store. I remember. She was ill. But not so bad. I remember her smile. Yes, yes, it looked like that. There. Just like you would imagine it. There. *(She turns to Andrea)* There is my mother's smile. Mother? Where have you been? I've been looking for you.

ANNA: Shut up! I am not your mother. Let's get back to work.

They start working again.

ANNA: *(struggles with the sail, stops, and looks out)* Where is my sister? She would know how I feel.

All stop working and look out into space.

CAROLINE: I remember her hands. Like the wings of a bird. There. *(She turns to Andrea)* There are my mother's hands. Mother? Where have you been? I've been looking for you. *(Andrea and Caroline begin to move in unison)*

MICHAEL: *(struggling with a piece of the mast)* My brother would be able to help me lift this.

CAROLINE: Yes, yes. She would move as lightly as a cat.

SARA: My father knew a work song.

CAROLINE: Like falling rain. I would never hear her footsteps.
GENIA: My friend could dance like the wind.
CAROLINE: As if a gentle hug was always on my shoulders.
JULIA: I remember.
CAROLINE: She is closer. She is. (*They stop moving*) She was with him at the store.
JULIA: I remember.

Bryna puts her arm around Caroline.

CAROLINE: She was sick.
BRYNA: Yes. She was sick.
CAROLINE: But not so bad.

Bryna, Caroline, Andrea, Genia, Julia, Miriam, Sara, and Anna sing.

Sister

Sometimes the rain will fall.
The ground will be hard on you.
No one's around to hear your call
To ease your fears
Or wipe the tears.
If there's anything I can do
I can be your sister.
I can take your hand.
I can be your guide
As you wander through the land.
I can be your sister
When the day is through.
I will be your sister.
I will care for you.

At the end of the song, Sebastian enters. He is very ill. He falls, calling out to Caroline.

SEBASTIAN: Mother.
CAROLINE: I can be your mother. (*She goes to Sebastian and comforts him*).
RACHEL: (*reading*) We learned to care for one another.

Everyone has stopped working. Ani stares up at the sky. Polina sees her and joins her, then Marc joins them. Then Josh, Julia, Lera, and Michael. They are all looking intently at the empty sky. Philip and Sabina walk around during the song trying to get them to go back to work. All of the members of the groups sing.

In the Sky

When I'm looking way up high
I can see up in the sky.
Big white clouds like ice cream cones.
I can taste berry scones.
Way up there everything seems
So much better in my dreams.
Looking at the sky.
Sometimes I can fly.

PHILIP: *(stops the singing with his voice)* Hey, what are you doing? Get back to work! *(Everyone ignores him and begins to sing again.)*

When I'm looking way up high
I can see in the sky.
Clouds like snow where candles glow.
Sailboats gently float.
Way up there everything seems
So much better in my dreams.
Looking at the sky.
Sometimes I just fly.

PHILIP: Stop! Stop! You must work. Work!

Slowly, everyone returns to their work on the ship, closer now and working together.

RACHEL: *(reading)* Sails, wings, and dreams for the future away from this world of pain kept us happy. The work was good.
KARIN: *(moves over to Rachel)* Yes, now was a good time.
RACHEL: *(to Karin)* It was a good time.
KARIN: Do you think this was right?
RACHEL: Do I think it was right?
KARIN: Do you think it was the correct thing to do? To escape.
RACHEL: How can they live on? When no one would take them in? When those that could help, didn't?

Karin hands her an orange.

Philip pulls Jonathan aside and confers with him. They compare the work with what is on the plan.

JONATHAN: Everybody listen up! The big guy says we need a few things. A lake for drinking.

ROMAN: *(looks at the ship, looks at the others, and shrugs)* Check.

JONATHAN: Oil for the engine.

BRONWYN: *(looks at the ship, looks at the others, and shrugs)* Check.

JONATHAN: An ocean for soup.

DENISE: *(looks at the ship, looks at the others, and shrugs)* I'll get one. *(She doesn't.)*

JONATHAN: A forest for the stove.

MIRIAM: *(looks at the ship, looks at the others, and shrugs)* Check.

JONATHAN: Good. *(looks at Philip)* That'll do it.

LERA: *(speaking in Russian, very fast)* No. It doesn't look correct. Something is most defiantly amiss. I can't put my finger on it. It's not so obvious like a mast or a rudder, but something is not there. Not right. Not there. Perhaps it's just a feeling that I have, but I don't think so. These feelings are universal don't you think?

JOSH: *(not really understanding)* I hear that. It's not quite there yet.

JULIA: She's right. It needs something.

MIRA: I think it needs a lady or something on the front.

EMILY: A figurehead?

LERA: That's it. A figurehead.

Lera, Josh, Emily, Julia, and Mira make a figurehead, which incorporates the items they picked up at the beginning of the play. Lera walks over and retrieves the pine cone and places it on the figurehead.

Everyone continues to put the ship together as they sing. During the song, the mast is raised and the sails are hoisted. They repeat the song until the ship is complete and ready to sail.

If Only

If only my imagination
Could make a better place
If only I can flee
And I can help me
Help me.
We can build a ship
We can build a plane

We can build an island
We can stop the pain
If only we believe
If only
If only we believe.

Everyone marvels at the sight of the ship they have created. Suddenly there is a bolt of lightning and a loud clap of thunder. The lights dim and everyone takes cover.

The chorus enters and sings.

Earth Is Calling You

Earth is calling you
Earth is calling you
Earth is calling you
Earth is calling you
You don't have to leave
Help us you still can
You don't have to leave
Just don't pollute this land
Earth, fire, ocean, sky
All we want to ask is why?
Why don't you stop why don't you change your ways?
Turn yourselves around
Change your yesterdays
Earth, fire, ocean, sky
All we want to ask is why.
Why?

The chorus exits, softly singing a repetition of the song. The lights brighten and everyone slowly comes out from their places.

Scene Three: Dreams for the Future

RACHEL: *(reading)* It was great day. The day of our departure
    from this world of troubles.
JONATHAN: Is everyone ready?

Caroline helps Sebastian onto the ship.

PHILIP: Are you sure we should take him?

She just looks at him and keeps going.

Everyone starts to load their things onto the ship, pantomiming the various objects and moving in rhythm with one another.

SABINA: What is that you're taking?
DENISE: My mother's tea set.
SABINA: And what is that?
MARGUERITA: A serving tray. It was a gift.
PHILIP: *(looking off stage right)* What is that?
BRYAN: It's a fifty-seven Chevy my brother rebuilt. Hey, I can't leave without it. *(he mimes lifting into the ship)*
SABRINA: Can someone help me with this hillside?
MIRIAM: *(helps her)* And snow. We need snow. I want to go sledding.
MONA: I'll bring the snow *(she mimes shoveling snow into the ship)*
SABRINA: Cool.

Ani and Polina mime loading a big box.

ANI: We've got six clouds in here. But we need another box for the rain.
POLINA: A waterproof box!
PHILIP: *(shouting)* Stop! Wait! What are you doing?
SABINA: Are you planning on taking the whole earth?
ALL: *(after a moment, in unison)* Well . . . yes! Sounds like a good idea. Of course. We must.
PHILIP: No. Stop! You can't.
ANI: *(looking in the box)* He's right. Look, the clouds slipped through the cracks.
BRYNA: If we can't take the earth, I don't want to go.
ILONA: She's right. We can't run away.
JENNY: We can't take the sun from the sky.
YURI: Even if it were possible, it wouldn't be right.

From offstage, we hear the chorus softly singing, "Earth Is Calling You."

SARA: I hear something. I heard it before.
EVERYONE: I do too. Me too. Do you hear that?

They all confer in a big huddle. Then break.

> BRYNA: *(acting as spokesperson for the whole group)* We've
> decided. We're not leaving.
> PHILIP: Fine. Then we go without you. Come.
> SABINA: *(She looks at Philip and then to the group)* No.

She walks away and joins the others. Philip, Nanette, and Karin are alone center stage.

> PHILIP: Well, this is fine. Then we will all stay.
> NANETTE: What are you doing? We must leave. Look, our
> beautiful ship is ready.
> PHILIP: Ask them!
> NANETTE: How can you live in this world of pain?

Karin touches her shoulder. She turns and sees Karin for the first time.

> NANETTE: Karin, my friend. How I've missed you.
> KARIN: I'm never far away. *(They hug one another)*
> RACHEL: *(reading)* I felt her strongly in that moment of decision.
> Asking me to stay, not to give up hope, to continue and
> live the simple dreams she and I had shared. A family, a
> home, a peaceful life.
> NANETTE: *(to Karin)* I feel so alone.
> RACHEL: *(reading)* I realized there was no cure for that in dis-
> tance or in time. *(She turns the page but discovers they are
> blank. She looks at Nanette.)* But wait. What did you decide
> to do? The pages are blank. Where is the end of the story?

Nanette takes the book from her, gently and without anger.

> RACHEL: What did you do?

Nanette and Karin walk up stage to the archway where they first entered.

> RACHEL: *(to Philip)* Did you build a new world?

Philip walks up stage to joins Nanette and Karin.

> RACHEL : What did you decide?
> NANETTE: *(places the book where it was at the beginning)* To give
> you our words.

She returns to Philip and Karin upstage. The others move into places around the stage as the following lines are spoken.

MONA: To give you our music.
SARA: To give you our eyes.
ANDREA: To give you our dance.
DAVID: To give you our hopes.
SABRINA: To give you our voice.
MARC: To give you our hearts.
SVETLANA: To give you our wishes.

Lera gives her the pinecone from the figurehead.

RACHEL: And what are your wishes?
AZIZI: Africa
TANIA: Asia
ILONA: Europe
JENNY: North America
ROWEN: Australia
JOSH: South America
ALL: United. With no more secrets. A place where we take less
   and give more.
YURI: A living world in which everyone is cared for.
ALONA: This dream comes to me every night. I am walking in
   the future. It will shine and everyone will not believe their
   eyes. Good toys, hospitals, houses, smiles. These dreams
   come to me every night. I am walking in the future. It is
   blooming as an orchard.
ALL: *(to Rachel)* And what is your wish?
RACHEL: To never have lived a day in vain.

They all agree that is a good wish and start to leave.

RACHEL: Wait! Wait! Who are you?
ALL: *(everyone stops and turns to look at her)* We are you.
   We live in you. You are our dreams. Remember. And live.

They turn and continue to exit. Rachel looks at Philip, Nanette, and Karin.
They smile and turn to exit. Rachel follows them off up stage.

Coda

The whole cast comes back on stage to sing the final song.

Boundless

Our fathers and mothers
Struggled in faith and in trust
That one day the guns of war would rust.
So rise up every daughter and son
The work has only just begun.
The dream of your parents is in your hands
Peace across all lands.
A boundless world.
An open heart.
An endless peace.
A place to start.
Our chance for peace
Has finally come.
A boundless earth.
A peaceful one.
Our courage must be great
The measure of our worth
Will be a boundless peace
Upon a boundless earth.

$\boxed{B}$ibliography and Resources

Included in this bibliography are books, articles, and resources useful for considering the work of a teaching artist. Many are quoted in this book. Others are sources of inspiration and ideas for teaching.

Education and Teaching

AIRASIAN, PETER W. 1996. *Assessment in the Classroom*. New York: McGraw-Hill.

AYERS, WILLIAM, ED. 1995. *To Become a Teacher: Making a Difference in Children's Lives*. New York: Teachers College, Columbia University.

BARTON, BOB, AND DAVID BOOTH. 1990. *Stories in the Classroom*. Portsmouth, NH: Heinemann.

BRUNER, JEROME S. 1960. *The Process of Education*. New York: Vintage Books.

CONNELLY, F. MICHAEL, AND D. JEAN CLANDININ. 1988. *Teachers As Curriculum Planners: Narratives of Experience*. New York: Teachers College, Columbia University.

DEWEY, JOHN. 1910/1991. *How We Think*. New York: Prometheus.

GAGE, N. L. 1978. *The Scientific Basis of the Art of Teaching*. New York: Teachers College Press.

GEHRKE, NATHALIE J. 1987. *On Being a Teacher*. West Lafayette, IN: Kappa Delta Pi.

GOODLAD, JOHN L. 1990. *Teachers for Our Nation's Schools*. San Francisco: Jossey-Bass.

GREENE, MAXINE. 1978. *Landscapes of Learning*. New York: Teachers' College, Columbia University.

————. 1991. "Teaching: The Question of Personal Reality." In *Staff Development for Education in the '90s: New Demands, New Realities, New Perspectives*, edited by Ann Lieberman and Lynn Miller. New York: Teachers College, Columbia University.

GROSSMAN, PAMELA L. 1990. *The Making of a Teacher: Teacher Knowledge and Teacher Education*. New York: Teachers College, Columbia University.

HOLLY, PETER. 1991. "Action Research: The Missing Link in the Creation of School as Centers of Inquiry." In *Staff Development for Education in the '90s: New Demands, New Realities, New Perspectives*, edited by Ann Lieberman and Lynn Miller. New York: Teachers College, Columbia University.

KOHL, HERBERT. 1984. *Growing Minds: On Becoming a Teacher*. New York: Harper and Row.

KOHN, ALFIE. 1998. *What to Look for in a Classroom and Other Essays*. San Francisco: Jossey-Bass.

KOUNIN, JACOB. 1970. *Discipline and Group Management in Classrooms*. New York: Holt, Rinehart and Winston.

LITTLE, JUDITH WARREN, AND MILBREY WALLIN MCLAUGHLIN, EDS. 1993. *Teachers' Work: Individuals, Colleagues, and Contexts*. New York: Teachers College, Columbia University.

LORTIE, DAN C. 1975. *Schoolteacher: A Sociological Study*. Chicago: University of Chicago Press.

National Commission on Excellence in Education. 1983. *A Nation at Risk: The Imperative for Educational reform: A Report to the Nation and the Secretary of Education, United States Department of Education*. Washington, DC: The Commission [Supt. of Docs., U.S.G.P.O. distributor].

OSTERMAN, K. 2000. "Students' Need for Belonging in the School Community." *Review of Educational Research* 70 (3): 323–367.

PIAZZA, CAROLYN L. 1999. *Multiple Forms of Literacy: Teaching Literacy and the Arts*. Columbus, OH: Merrill.

SARASON, SEYMOUR B. 1999. *Teaching as a Performing Art*. New York: Teachers College, Columbia University.

SCHÖN, DONALD. 1983. *The Reflective Practitioner.* New York: Basic Books.

SHULMAN, LEE S. 1986. "Paradigms and Research Programs in the Study of Teaching: A Contemporary Perspective." In *Handbook of Research on Teaching*, edited by Merlin C. Wittrock. New York: Macmillan.

————. 1987. "Knowledge and Teaching: Foundations of the New Reform." *Harvard Educational Review* 57 (1): 1–21.

U.S. Congress. House. 2001. *No Child Left Behind Act of 2001 (NCLB),* 107th Cong., 1st sess. HR 1, P.L. 107–110. *www.ed.gov/nclb* (accessed July 20, 2005).

WILSON, SUZANNE M., WITH CAROL MILLER AND CAROL YERKES. 1993. "Deeply Rooted Change: A Tale of Learning to Teach Adventurously." In *Teaching for Understanding: Challenges for Policy and Practice,* edited by David K. Cohen, Milbrey McLaughlin, and Joan E. Talbert. San Francisco: Jossey-Bass.

Arts Education

BOOTH, ERIC. 2003. "Seeking Definition: What Is a Teaching Artist?" *Teaching Artist Journal* 1 (1): 5–12.

———. 2004. "Improving the Quality of the Artists' Residency Programs: A Rubric for Teaching Artists." *Teaching Artist Journal* 2 (4): 212–26.

CHAPMAN, LAURA H. 2004. "No Child Left Behind in Art?" *Arts Education Policy Review* 106 (2): 3–17.

COOPER, LYNN. 2004. "Participation: Who Comes to What and Why." *Teaching Artist Journal* 2 (1): 58–60.

DAVIS, JESSICA HOFFMAN. 2005. *Framing Education As Art: The Octopus Has a Good Day.* New York: Teachers College, Columbia University.

DEASY, RICHARD J., ED. 2002. *Critical Links: Learning in the Arts and Student Academic and Social Development.* Washington, DC: Arts Education Partnership.

EISNER, ELIOT W. 1971. "How Can You Measure a Rainbow? Tactics for Evaluating the Teaching of Art." *Art Education* 24 (5): 36–9.

ELSTER, ANGELA. 2001. "Learning Through the Arts: Program Goals, Features, and Pilot Results." *International Journal of Education and the Arts* 2 (7). *http://ijea.asu.edu/v2n7/* (accessed June 20, 2005).

FINEBERG, CAROL, ed. 2002. *Planning an Arts-Centered School: A Handbook.* New York: Dana Foundation.

GARDNER, HOWARD. 1983. *Frames of Mind: The Theory of Multiple Intelligences.* New York: Basic Books.

———. 1996. "The Assessment of Student Learning in the Arts." In *Evaluating and Assessing the Visual Arts in Education: International Perspectives,* edited by Doug Broughton, Elliot W. Eisner, and Johan Ligtvoet. New York: Teachers College, Columbia University.

GOLDBERG, MERRYL, ED. 2004. *Teaching English Language Learners through the Arts: A SUAVE Experience*. Boston: Allyn and Bacon.

GREENE, MAXINE. 1995. *Releasing the Imagination: Essays on Education, the Arts, and Social Change*. San Francisco: Jossey-Bass.

HEATH, SHIRLEY BRICE, WITH ADELMA ROACH. 1999. "Imaginative Actuality: Learning in the Arts during Nonschool Hours." In *Champions of Change: The Impact of the Arts on Learning*, edited by Edward B. Fiske. Washington, DC: Arts Education Partnership.

MADEJA, STANLEY S. 2004. "Alternative Assessment for Schools." *Arts Education Policy Review* 105 (5): 3–13.

MANDELL, JAN, AND JENNIFER LYNN WOLF. 2003. *Acting, Learning, and Change: Creating Original Plays with Adolescents*. Portsmouth, NH: Heinemann.

MAY, ROLLO. 1975. *The Courage to Create*. New York: W. W. Norton.

MEBEN, MARGARET. 2002. "The Postmodern Artist in the School: Implications for Arts Partnership Programs." *International Journal of Education and the Arts* 3 (1). http://ijea.asu.edu/v3n1/ (accessed January 20, 2005).

National Endowment for the Arts. 1988. *Toward Civilization: Overview from a Report on Arts Education*. Washington, DC: The Endowment.

NORMAN, JANIA. 2004. "Improving the Quality of the Artists' Residency Programs: A Rubric for Teaching Artists." *Teaching Artist Journal* 2 (4): 212–26.

REMER, JANE. 1996. *Beyond Enrichment: Building Effective Arts Partnerships with Schools and Your Community*. New York: ACA Books American Council on the Arts.

SABOL, F. ROBERT. 2004. "The Assessment Context: Part Two." *Arts Education Policy Review* 105 (4): 3–9.

STAKE, ROBERT. 1975. *Evaluating the Arts in Education*. Columbus, OH: Charles E. Merrill.

Theatre

ACKROYD, JUDITH. 2000. "Applied Theatre: Problems and Possibilities." *Applied Theatre Researcher* 1 (1). *http://www.griffith.edu.au/centre/cpci /atr/* (accessed June 14, 2004).

ARISTOTLE. 1977. *Poetics*. Translated by Gerald F. Else. Ann Arbor, MI: University of Michigan Press.

BOAL, AUGUSTO. 1979. *Theatre of the Oppressed*. Translated by Charles A. and Maria-Odelia Leal McBride. New York: Theatre Communications Group.

BROOK, PETER. 1968. *The Empty Space*. New York: Atheneum.

GROTOWSKI, JERZY. 1968. *Towards a Poor Theatre*. New York: Simon and Schuster.

JOHNSTONE, KEITH. 1981. *Impro: Improvisation and the Theatre*. New York: Routledge.

KERRIGAN, SHEILA. 2001. *The Performer's Guide to the Collaborative Process*. Portsmouth, NH: Heinemann.

SCHECHNER, RICHARD. 1973. *Environmental Theatre*. New York: Hawthorn Books.

SMILEY, SAM. 1971. *Playwriting: The Structure of Action*. Englewood Cliffs, NJ: Prentice-Hall.

SMITH, HAZEL, AND ROGER DEAN. 1997. *Improvisation, Hypermedia and the Arts since 1945*. Australia: Harwood Academic Publishers.

TURNER, VICTOR. 1982. *From Ritual to Theatre: The Human Seriousness of Play*. New York: PAJ Publications.

WRIGHT, MICHAEL. 1997. *Playwriting in Process: Thinking and Working Theatrically*. Portsmouth, NH: Heinemann.

Theatre Education

BOAL, AUGUSTO. 1992. *Games for Actors and Non-Actors*. Translated by Adrian Jackson. NewYork: Routledge.

BRAY, ERROL. 1991. *Playbuilding: A Guide for Group Creation of Plays with Young People*. Portsmouth, NH: Heinemann.

CHAPMAN, GERALD. 1991. *Teaching Young Playwrights*. Portsmouth, NH: Heinemann.

DOYLE, REX. 2003. *Staging Youth Theatre*. Ramsbury, England: Crowood.

GATTENHOF, SANDRA. 2004. "The Poetics of Deterritorialization: A Motivating Force in Contemporary Youth Performance." *Youth Theatre Journal* 18: 122–37.

GRADY, SHARON. 2000. *Drama and Diversity: A Pluralistic Perspective for Educational Drama*. Portsmouth, NH: Heinemann.

HEATHCOATE, DOROTHY. 1984. *Collected Writings on Education and Drama*. Edited by Liz Johnson and Cecily O'Neill. Evanston, IL: Northwestern University Press.

HORNBROOK, DAVID, ED. 1998. *On the Subject of Drama*. London: Routledge.

HUGHES, CATHERINE. 1998. *Museum Theatre: Communicating with Visitors Through Drama*. Portsmouth, NH: Heinemann.

JOHNSTON, CHRIS. 1998. *House of Games: Making Theatre from Everyday Life*. New York: Routledge.

JOHNSTONE, KEITH. 1999. *Impro for Storytellers*. New York: Routledge.

KEMPE, ANDY. 2000. "'So Whose Idea Was That, Then?': Devising Drama." In *Teaching Drama 11–18*, edited by Helen Nicholson. New York: Continuum, 64–76.

KOHL, HERBERT R. 1988. *Making Theatre: Developing Plays with Young People*. New York: Teachers and Writers Collaborative.

MANLEY, ANITA, AND CECILY O'NEILL. 1997. *Dreamseekers: Creative Approaches to the African American Heritage*. Portsmouth, NH: Heinemann.

NEELANDS, JONOTHAN. 1984. *Making Sense of Drama*. London: Heinemann.

NICHOLSON, HELEN, ED. 2000. *Teaching Drama 11–18*. London: Continuum.

ORECK, BARRY, SUSAN BAUM, AND STEVEN OWEN. 2004. "Assessment of Potential Theatre Arts Talent in Young People: The Development of a New Research-Based Assessment Process." *Youth Theatre Journal* 18: 146–63.

ROHD, MICHAEL. 1998. *Theatre for Community, Conflict and Dialogue: The Hope Is Vital Training Manual*. Portsmouth, NH: Heinemann.

SPOLIN, VIOLA. 1963. *Improvisation for the Theatre: A Handbook of Teaching and Directing Techniques*. Evanston, IL: Northwestern University Press.

———. 1985. *Theatre Games for Rehearsal: A Director's Handbook*. Evanston, IL: Northwestern University Press.

———.1986. *Improvisation for the Classroom*. Evanston, IL: Northwestern University Press.

TAYLOR, PHILIP. 2003. *Applied Theatre: Creating Transformative Encounters in the Community*. Portsmouth, NH: Heinemann.

WEIGLER, WILL. 2001. *Strategies for Playbuilding*. Portsmouth, NH: Heinemann.

Project Resources

BERSON, MISHA. "Kids Act Out for Peace." *Seattle Times*, 10 July 1992. TEMPO, 14.

CORSI, EDWARD. 1935. *In the Shadow of Liberty: The Chronicle of Ellis Island*. New York: Macmillan.

Diamonds: A Musical Revue. 1986. The Baseball Project Company. New York: Samuel French.

GESNER, CLARK. 1967. *You're a Good Man, Charlie Brown*. New York: Random House.

GORDON, PETER H., ED. 1987. *Diamonds Are Forever: Artists and Writers on Baseball*. San Francisco: Chronicle.

KINSELLA, W. P. 1982. *Shoeless Joe*. New York: Ballantine.

———. 1986. *The Iowa Baseball Conspiracy*. New York: Ballantine.

LORD, BETTY BAO. 1984. *In the Year of the Boar and Jackie Robinson*. New York: HarperTrophy.

PARKER, W. 1989. "Trends: Social Studies, Reading, and Writing (and Singing and Dancing) to Learn About Immigration." *Educational Leadership* 47 (2).

SIMON, NEIL. 1984. *Brighton Beach Memoirs*. New York: Samuel French.

THAYER, E. L. 1967. "Casey at the Bat." In *The Annotated Casey at the Bat: A Collection of Ballads about the Mighty Casey*, edited by Martin Gardner. New York: C. N. Potter.

ZOGLIN, RICHARD. 2004. "Setting a New Stage for Kids." *Time Magazine*, 15 November 2004. *http://www.time.com/time/archive/preview/0,10987, 995622,00.html* (accessed November 20, 2004).

/Index